THAT'S ENTERTAINMENT

RICK BUCKLER

MY LIFE IN THE JAM

THAT'S
ENTERTAINMENT

RICK
BUCKLER

MY LIFE IN THE JAM

OMNIBUS PRESS

London / New York / Paris / Sydney / Copenhagen / Berlin / Madrid / Tokyo

Cover designed by Fresh Lemon
Picture research by Rick Buckler

ISBN: 978.1.78558.640.8
Order No: OP57486

Exclusive Distributors
Music Sales Limited,
14/15 Berners Street,
London, W1T 3LJ.

Music Sales Corporation
180 Madison Avenue, 24th Floor,
New York,
NY 10016,
USA.

Macmillan Distribution Services
56 Parkwest Drive
Derrimut, Vic 3030,
Australia.

Every effort has been made to trace the copyright holders of the photographs in this book but one or
two were unreachable. We would be grateful if the photographers concerned would contact us.

Printed in the EU.

A catalogue record for this book is available from the British Library.

Visit Omnibus Press on the web at www.omnibuspress.com

Acknowledgements

A special thank you to my wife, Lesley, also Jason and Holly
for being there and to my Mum and Dad.

With thanks to Snowy, Tony Fletcher, Barry Cain and Barry Rutter.
Mark Melton for his sound advice. Also SME Protect Insurance Brokers.
Michael and Christine Perkins from The Hare and Hounds for their
patience and generous hospitality.

For the use of the photographs:
Twink (Official photographer for The Jam 1980–82)
Derek D'Souza (www.absoluteluck.co.uk)
Danielle Tunstall (www.danielletunstall.com)
David Lees
Tim V
Tony Briggs

Dedication

To my dear friend Jimmy Edwards, RIP

FOREWORD

By Tony Fletcher

As one-third of The Jam, Rick Buckler was more than just the group's phenomenally accomplished and historically under-rated drummer. He was more than just the man at the back. His role was central, his view un-obscured. On stage, Paul Weller always stood off to his right, and Bruce Foxton off to his left, and that allowed Rick to remain focused straight ahead. Both on stage and off, Rick Buckler grounded the band. For while Paul and Bruce each possessed ego in the large quantities necessary to make it in the music business, especially for a band swept along by (but not truly representative of) the punk rock explosion, Rick, by comparison, appeared to be blessedly free of it. He was, certainly, no less fiercely proud of The Jam's accomplishments – musical, critical and commercial – but he never seemed to get caught up in the whole rock'n'roll circus, the personality issues and confrontations that typically become part and parcel of every musically aggressive young band. As such, if he didn't necessarily seek out a role as peacemaker, he established it by example.

Fans came to know as much. The Jam, to the legions of followers who took them from supposed punk-rock has-beens in 1978 to the top of the charts in 1980, where they stayed, more or less, until their break-up at the end of 1982, were always very much a three-piece. It was Paul, Bruce *and* Rick that made the group such a frightening proposition on stage and such an enticing one in the studio, and fans were rarely any less honoured to sit and talk with Rick after a soundcheck, or outside a venue at the end of the night; it was just that Rick seemed no less honoured to be talking with the fans.

He was equally casual when it came to clothes. For the acolytes who, however much they might splurge, couldn't possibly hope to emulate Weller's innately stylish nature (and that was pretty much all of them), Buckler offered an alternative. His relaxed personality frequently manifested itself in relaxed but ineffably sharp fashion. Rick was the everyman's mod.

All good things must come to an end though, some more prematurely than others, and when Weller called time on The Jam in the late summer of 1982, Buckler, like Foxton, was caught short. Perhaps not comfortable joining an established band – though he certainly would have been first choice on many a rock group's list - he set about forming The Time (shortly to become The Time UK), before moving into studio and band management. He never, however, lost his musical chops. When he decided to resume playing the band's songs onstage, in the early 2000s, in a group that morphed from the name The Gift to From The Jam as it briefly included Foxton in its ranks, he demonstrated that he had lost none of the dexterity, nor the sheer athleticism and stamina that had always won admiration from the fans. Proof of Buckler's prowess as a powerhouse, if you really need the evidence, is evident in the studio introduction to 'All Around The World', the mid-section of 'Strange Town', the fierce finale to 'Down In The Tube Station At Midnight' and through pretty much every beat of 'Funeral Pyre'. His subtleties may be less apparent, but only because they were so effective.

Throughout it all, Rick has kept his cool. He has never lashed out as his former front man, never exhibited bitterness or rancour at the unexpected break-up of the finest band in a generation. As should be evident from the pages that follow, Buckler is something you don't encounter every day: a true gent, in the finest sense of the word.

Tony Fletcher is the author of *Dear Boy: The Life of Keith Moon* and *Boy About Town*, among other books.

INTRODUCTION

There have been many books written about The Jam, my memories are of a working band enjoying the music and the gigs, working hard and finding success and satisfaction in what we did; then coming to terms with the reality of that achievement.

By the time Paul Weller announced that he wanted to leave The Jam during that interview for *Nationwide*, it was already old news to Bruce and me. I never actually saw that interview at the time, when it was broadcast, but I've watched it since and it doesn't make sense. The thing that struck me immediately was that several months earlier, when Paul told us that he wanted to leave the band, the reason he gave was different to what he said in that interview. The interviewer asked the question: 'The band has been amazingly successful, why stop now?' and Paul replied: 'I feel we have achieved enough, I think we have done all we can do as the three of us, I think it's a good time to finish. I don't want to drag it on for the next 20 years and become nothing, mean nothing like all the other groups. I want this to count for something.'

None of us were happy with Paul's decision, not our fans, not me, not Bruce, and not his dad, John Weller, who was also our manager. We had all put so much work and commitment into the band that in so many ways it felt The Jam was actually coming to fruition. We had proven ourselves as a band to the industry, we were a band that could get number one records, we could sell albums, do world tours and we had a strong and loyal fanbase. We had achieved so much. OK, we could have done some extra work in America or explored new territories such as China or Russia, but generally speaking we had broken the back of what we were about, as a British three-piece band.

In 1982 we were no longer struggling against the industry like we were in the early days when the pressure was all about how many albums we could sell. We spent years having to answer that and prove that we were something outstanding. It was those pressures from the record company that had made us work so hard during the five years that we were signed to Polydor. Yet, despite all this we had not succumbed to commercial influences or rested on our laurels; we still had our integrity.

The Jam was also only just starting to earn some real money. We had just got to the point where we could tour America without having to ask for tour support. Up until that time, most of the money that we earned went straight back into the band. When the record company gave us an advance it got absorbed into paying for tour support, studio costs and hotels. As a result of this we never really earned any money. Then, by 1982 this was beginning to change and we were starting to see some pretty green. It was different for Paul because he earned money from songwriting through his publishing company, but this wasn't the case for Bruce and me. But yes, the band certainly did mean something important to us and many other people, and I felt that there was so much more we could do together, as The Jam.

That morning we had all arrived to record some demos at Red Bus Studio. We had all been on our summer holidays and Bruce and I were in good spirits. Plus we always enjoyed studio time, which was a welcome break from being on the road, which, although equally enjoyable, was a change too. John was already there and told Bruce and me that we were having a group meeting. We never had meetings, so this sounded ominous to start with. Paul sat next to

John and opposite Bruce, and I sat next to Bruce in the foyer of the studio. Then John said that Paul had something he needed to say. Paul, prompted by John, explained that he felt he was on a treadmill, dictated by our contractual obligations with Polydor and just going around and around. This I fully understood. Being in The Jam felt like that to all three of us. When a band is signed to a label it's part of the deal to supply the record company with product and promote the product with tours and interviews. I think Paul felt that he was being forced to write songs to order, writing to fulfil contracts and no longer able to do things that he and Bruce and myself wanted to. In summary Paul told us he was leaving The Jam.

It came as a shock. I felt gutted that Paul had decided to leave the band and for those reasons. We all felt that we understood how Paul was feeling, but unfortunately nobody turned around and told the record company that we weren't going to continue like that. All of us should have spoken up. John, as our manager, should have spoken up, especially as we had finally got into a position where we could, to some extent, call the shots. I loved John to bits, especially for all he had done for us in the early days, but I don't think he really grasped what was happening at the time.

We didn't speak up and we didn't break the cycle, that self-inflicted treadmill that we had been on for five years. As a band we really did work hard during those years, always on the road or in the studio and in the end Paul just said, 'I've had enough.' I remember Bruce saying to Paul: 'Why don't we just stop for six months or a year even? Let's take stock of our lives; we can afford to do this now.' We even said it was OK if Paul wanted to go off and do something else, like a solo project or something. But Paul had made his mind up. It was the end of The Jam.

However, when the announcement was made on *Nationwide*, the reason Paul had given us had changed, with little resemblance to what he had told us back in the summer. So by the time the announcement was made I felt that Paul was trying to justify his decision in some way to the public and the fans. In that *Nationwide* interview he also added: 'It's something I felt inside me, and I just got to go by instinct and I felt it was the right thing to do.' I was hearing something new.

We had often talked amongst ourselves about the possible demise of the band, and the subject had come up a few times in press interviews, so we understood that nothing – and especially a group – lasts forever. The reasons for any group having to call it a day are varied and often unexpected. But to give up and throw away what we had achieved, at that time, left us with the impression that only Paul thought it had gone wrong in some way.

My view was that the band did already mean something. We had built a great relationship with our fans. We had produced and written songs that people loved and could relate to. What we felt and thought, they felt and thought too. I felt that Paul had missed the point in some way and Paul's decision just didn't seem to add up. Everyone tried to dissuade Paul, me, Bruce, John, the record company, everyone, but it was too late.

Then there was the issue that we hadn't actually fulfilled our present record contract and, because there was no way we were going to make another studio album, the label hurriedly put together *Dig The New Breed*. We had loads of live recordings, but looking back I don't think *Dig The New Breed* was the best thought-out album or that it selected the best live recordings available. There was nothing wrong with the songs, but a lot wrong with its hurried production. The *Live Jam* album that was released much later is a much better collection of live songs. Most of my memories of being in The Jam are about being on stage playing live, so the live recordings still mean more to me personally.

Another thing about those record label contracts is that they never really come to an end. There's always options to pick up. I heard many years later that Paul had signed a contract with Polydor for the Style Council some months before The Jam played their last show. So it seems Paul jumped off of one treadmill and straight onto another one anyway.

Paul originally wanted to keep his departure from us until the end of the last tour that year, but was wisely advised against this and to do the right thing. Once Paul had told Bruce and me what he had decided, what we did was agree that we would finish things properly. We already had some shows arranged in advance anyway. There was no special reason for that tour; we had no planned product being released, no album or single. But once it became the final tour extra dates started to get added in and we started to think about what we should do for the final show and where we should have it.

The shows at Wembley were added to the tour. They started out as a couple of dates then the promoter contacted us and said: 'We've sold out. We need to add another date' and then another was added and we ended up doing five nights at Wembley. We had to put our foot down and say, 'Stop, we're not adding any more shows. We have to draw a line under this somewhere.'

Not that we were not looking forward to the shows at Wembley, we were, we were looking forward to them a lot. One of the things that The Jam loved to do was tour and play live; it always gave us a real good buzz; it's what we were about. We were a live band, I think more so than a studio band. I remember the soundcheck at Wembley. The place was cavernous and empty; well apart from a couple of hundred people milling about, but it still felt empty.

And throughout all this time there was still this small hope that Paul might change his mind, but he didn't and we were professional to the end. In fact, playing wise, I think that last tour was the best tour that we did; everybody shone. It was a strange feeling, but like we always did, we put our hearts and souls into it.

Then the time arrived to play the last show at the Brighton Conference Centre. One thing that vividly sticks in my mind is reading the set list that I used to have taped to my bass drum. I remember going through the songs and reading the set list, ticking off song by song, and about halfway through the show I suddenly realised that this was probably the last time I would ever be playing those numbers. I remember thinking, as each song passed, that this will be the last time, and then this will be the last time. And then by the end of the set, we played 'The Gift' and that was that, it was all gone, as if the end of The Jam was being played out on a set list.

It was very strange and in some ways it didn't seem real. I couldn't understand how this situation of The Jam splitting up had come about. Only five years before we could only have dreamed of playing the types of shows that we were doing. And it was like, 'What the fuck's going on?'

For me, playing big shows hadn't been any different to playing little shows – it's only the scenery that changes. When I'm playing drums I'm still doing the same job. Some of those venues, such as Wembley or Brighton, were huge and when you look out you can't see the people at the back but then we had played the Nashville and Red Cow, so many years earlier, and we could see all the people. But the gig was still the same. The Jam still played the same.

The atmosphere from the audience at the last show in Brighton was really tense. I could see faces just staring up at us. People looked almost mannequin-like, as if it hadn't really sunk in that that was to be the final Jam show. We had a special relationship with the fans and I still get this today, and I'm sure Paul and Bruce do too. People say we, The Jam, belonged to them and we did, and they the fans belonged to us in the same way. It was something we all felt. That was something special about The Jam. I really liked that connection. I liked that there was no 'them and us'. Often an attitude and behaviour exists with so many bands where they don't mix with their fans and they put up a huge barrier. This wasn't us. The Jam just wasn't like that at all.

Yes, there was a very strange atmosphere on that night in Brighton. Once we finished playing the last song someone grabbed me and said you should say something to the audience. Before that point I had never spoken on stage through a microphone. I had no idea what to say and I was completely unprepared. I don't remember what I said; those few moments remain a blur to me. In fact I don't have many memories about the rest of the night. There was certainly no after-party; there may have been a few drinks back at the Grand Hotel, drinking was The Jam's number one sport, but it really felt like me, Bruce and Paul simply walked away from The Jam.

I think The Jam's last Christmas party (at the Greyhound in Fulham) may have even happened before the final show. And that was very different to how they had been. It felt very separate and disconnected. It was as if three different parties were being held in the same room. We had held Christmas parties for the last three years of The Jam. All the crew, people from the record company, agents, promoters, family members and so on would come. It was like a big works do.

It wasn't until I was sitting alone at home, during that Christmas period, that I took stock really. For years, since school, The Jam had been such a big part of my life, a matter of getting up in the morning and having something to look forward to, there was always somewhere to travel to or something the band had to do. But now it felt like I was unemployed. I didn't know what I wanted to do. I had no plans in place. Only then did it all really sink in and it felt like I was standing on the edge of a chasm. I had no idea what to do. I could do this or I could try that, I could start a new band up. but they all seemed like foggy ideas and a far cry from the sort of concrete reality that I had been used to, since 1974, when I first became one of the founding members of The Jam which, as John Weller used to yell as he announced us on stage, was 'the best fuckin' band in the world'.

CHAPTER ONE

I was born Paul Richard Buckler on December 6, 1955. Bill Haley's 'Rock Around The Clock' was at the top of the Christmas tree in the *Record Mirror* charts. To take my mother's mind off the huge bump in her belly, in the months leading up to my arrival, the airwaves had mostly been filled with Dean Martin, Frankie Laine and Tony Bennett. My own toddler years were dominated by the slightly sexier sounds of Elvis, Tommy Steele and Jerry Lee Lewis. Not that I knew or even cared, but I may have cracked a dribbling smile at the sound of my mother humming along to those not so innocent tunes. However those songs were very far removed from the sort of songs that I would find myself drumming along to, on stage with Paul Weller and Bruce Foxton some two decades later.

The significance for teenagers of songs like 'Rock Around The Clock' and rock'n'roll in general evoked energies and emotions parallel with what The Jam got caught up in around 1977, after 'In The City' was released. The explosion of punk was the second most important thing that had happened to teenagers since the rock'n'roll assault that the punks' mothers and fathers had witnessed… and us three young men from Woking dared to be a part of.

I certainly hadn't seen me playing drums in a punk band some 20 years earlier when I was born in the local maternity hospital in Woking that December of '55. Mind you, there are far worse places to have been born. Woking in west Surrey falls within the London commuter belt, just 24 minutes by train from Waterloo Station. The town is surrounded by several villages that include Sheerwater, Maybury and Westfield and is proud of its multi-cultural community, mostly made up of Pakistani, Irish and Italian families. Up until the fifties Woking was the pre-eminent centre of Islam in the UK. It even gets a mention in the Domesday Book, the kind of place that has never been overlooked yet one that doesn't especially stand out.

That said, Woking is a town that can name-drop one or two famous and important people (outside of The Jam that is). For example, HG Wells moved to 143 Maybury Road, Woking, after marrying his second wife, Amy Catherine Robbins, and while living there wrote *The War Of The Worlds* between 1895 and 1897, and today the Woking Martian in the town centre celebrates that important literary work. Not far away is the seven and a half ton three-pronged oak sculpture called 'The Space Between', sculpted by Richard Heys and intended as a tribute to The Jam, each prong representing one of the three members of the band. It was almost a year in the making, Richard Heys drew his inspiration not only from the band itself but also from local school children's interpretation of the group's music during workshops at St John the Baptist School, the renamed Bishop David Brown School that was previously called Sheerwater Comprehensive and Woking High School. I was invited, along with Paul and Bruce, to unveil the sculpture on July 12, 2012. I was disappointed that neither Paul nor Bruce showed up, although Paul did send a short message.

Other notable people with connections to Woking include the comedians Harry Hill and Sean Lock, musicians Rick Parfitt of Status Quo and Peter Cox of Go West and the town can also boast having its own Doctor Who – Peter Davison.

Up until a few years ago the Brookwood Cemetery, also known as the London Necropolis or the city of the dead, just outside of

Woking's town centre, was the largest in the world, and remains the largest in the UK. It also contributes to a small bit of Jam history. Paul Weller carved his name into one of the bricks in the old wall that surrounds the cemetery. This may act as an enjoyable, if not time consuming quest should any Jam fans be interested enough to try and find it. It's still there.

Nowadays, Woking, like mostly every other British town is virtually unrecognisable to those who had made the town their home. For Jam fans the town still represents an important part of the Jam story, and indeed it does have its place in that story. The streets, shops, pubs, schools, youth clubs and discos contributed to each Jam member's experience of growing up and ultimately their personalities. This Woking connection is something that seems to continue to intrigue Jam fans. The point was proven further when two of the band's oldest friends, Steve Carver and Sam Molnar, organised Jam tours around the town, as part of Vic Falsetta's Wake Up Woking charity event that he tied in with the promotion and launch of the Jam book *Thick As Thieves* by Ian Snowball and Stu Deabill in 2012. While I was sitting in Woking's Waterstones signing copies of *Thick As Thieves* with Stu and Snowy, Steve and Sam had hired a minibus and were driving around the town showing Jam fans such locations as the Woking Working Men's Club, Sheerwater School, Stanley Road and where Michaels once used to be. It was a well-received idea and helped put a few more quid into the fund-raiser bucket.

So Woking was my home town (it still is my nearest town) and this is where I spent a large part of my youth. I have many memories linked with the town, my friends and my family, but for me Christmas time is associated with some of my earliest memories. I have three brothers, John is the eldest, Andrew is next and then there is Peter, my twin. I didn't see much of John when I was growing up because he was always going to college and then to university. He trained to be a teacher and went on to become a head of department. And so because John was doing these things I don't remember him being in my youth very much. But Christmas was a time when the whole family would gather together.

Our family home was a three-bedroom terrace house at 14 Church Street. Even then it was quite a dilapidated building. There was no central heating, we had an outside toilet and to bathe ourselves we had to use a tin bath placed in front of the open fire. It's funny to think about that now and I have to remind myself that this was not that long ago. There was a sense of desperation around the house, for example the sash windows didn't fit properly and because of this they rattled when the wind blew. There was also damp in the walls. Our house was just one of many old terrace houses in Woking at that time. Many of those buildings have now been demolished and erased from Woking's once Victorian landscape.

The layout of our house was typical of its time. We would walk through the front door and the staircase would be in front of us. The front room was to the left and that had a bay window. We called this room the 'good room' and that was where all the best, yet conservative furniture was kept. It was the room we spent least time in. The next room was the dining room and this led to the kitchen where most of the house's activity went on. My parents slept in the bedroom at the front of the house, my older brother Andrew had the middle room and I shared the room at the back with my twin brother, Peter. We had no real loft to speak of and the staircase was almost vertical and sometimes tricky to climb. My parents liked to surround the house with pictures of the family posing at the seaside or on someone's birthday.

We did eventually get central heating, courtesy of my uncle Ted, and we did eventually knock out the coalhole at the back of our house and convert this into a bathroom that boasted an indoor loo. I also remember when we got our first mod cons such as a washing machine and television. But even then the radio was still king for a long while. At first we had a black and white TV, but there were still times when I would go around to my mate's house in Horsell to watch his family's colour TV, housed in a grand mahogany cabinet. The first thing I recall seeing was the movie *Fantastic Voyage*. It was a very exciting experience.

We had a traditional family setup in many ways. My dad worked hard and, being keen on DIY, did much to decorate the place. He would do all the wallpapering and general maintenance. He was also a good gardener and when he was young, before he went on to work for British Rail, worked at some big house as their gardener. Our garden had a little bit of lawn and a few flowers and a typical concrete post for the washing line. As kids we loved our garden. We had a swing in it, from which we would constantly be falling off and cracking our heads open. There was a small shed, which was really just a place to keep the rubbish out of the house. We were allowed in the shed, as long as we didn't touch anything. My dad valued his tools. My brother and I got a bike each one Christmas. We were allowed to keep our bikes in the shed and tinker around with them, adjusting the brakes and things. But on the whole the shed was our dad's place of retreat.

Being in a row of terraces meant that when you looked over the neighbours' garden fence you could see they were all pretty much the same. Additionally there was a strange affair in that there were gates that ran through all the back gardens. This meant that if you wanted, you could walk through everyone else's gardens (and if you so desired peer through their windows). Having this arrangement also meant that when the neighbours visited they would use the back garden entrance rather than the front door.

Back then we knew all the neighbours. There was a sense of community. There was a Scottish family at the end; then, next door to us was a Welshman who ran the local barbers and further along there were a couple of old spinsters. There was a builder family, the Timpsons, and I had an aunt that lived in the terraced houses across the road. Plus the Percy Street Baptist Church was just around the corner and the ABC cinema was a short walk away. It was a close-knit community really that we all took for granted.

As time passed sections of the street did fall prey to the dreams of council planners and the wrecking ball. One area was demolished and what remained was used as a car park for a while. I recall Messerschmitt bubble cars being parked in there. Someone was using the patch as a temporary car lot to sell second hand vehicles. I was quite fascinated that they were called Messerschmitts. I had grown up hearing stories of the Second World War and I knew that what was parked in that car park weren't real Messerschmitts.

Behind our house, at the bottom of the garden, were other gardens that belonged to another row of terrace houses on Goldsworth Road. In that street were located the nearest shops, including a toyshop called Ashplants, a great place for us kids to hang out and marvel at the toys. The big toys of the day were Scalextric and Hornby train sets, and there were board games and Airfix toy soldiers, which we would paint using small tins of Humbrol with their distinct smell because of the thinners in them. Airfix models were also just coming in and I spent a lot of time constructing, painting and eventually playing with them (briefly). The thing was, once I had constructed and painted them I didn't want to play with them because I didn't want them getting all grubby and roughed up.

Peter and I did inherit some toys from our older brothers, but not many. There was such an age difference between us, also being a twin meant we usually got two of everything. We certainly didn't get any hand-me-down clothes because Andrew was seven years older than us, and John even older than that.

Next door to the toy shop there was a sweet shop that would give you a deposit back for pop bottles. So we would collect discarded pop bottles and with the few pence we got we would buy ourselves a chocolate bar. There were only a few shops close to us so if we wanted anything else we had to walk into Woking, which was only a five-minute walk away. Woking had proper old-fashioned shops then, like fishmongers, grocers and fish and chips shops. Mind you, for some reason (that I don't recall ever being explained) the only time we really got fish and chips was on holiday.

Dad's name was Joseph William Buckler but everyone called him Bill. Before the Second World War he worked on the railways. This meant that when the war came along he was drafted into the Royal Engineers. He was in the 8th Army and spent a considerable chunk of the war fighting his way back and forth across North Africa.

Once the war was over he returned to Blighty and became a postman. Working for the GPO was a good job back then, although not particularly well paid and so he had to do plenty of overtime. When I was a bit older I heard stories that many Post Office shift workers used to take Purple Hearts in the sixties to help get them through the extra hours. It was hard physical work, up early with many hours spent on his feet, walking the streets of Woking in all weathers. So when the opportunity of a new job with the British Telecom Engineers came up he grabbed it.

Telephones were becoming more commonplace in people's homes and there was an increasing demand for engineers to install them. At first we had what was called a 'party line' in our house. This was shared with next door, an odd setup really. People would ring up and ask for somebody, but that somebody would often be the neighbour, so you would have to let them know somehow. It was a cheaper system, but one that gradually, and thankfully, fell out of favour. Plus if the neighbour was on their phone we could listen to their conversation on our hand set. But I didn't do this… much!

Everyone called my mum Peggy (short for Primrose). She was born in 1920. Her maiden name was White and her family were Woking based. She was a typical mum in many ways, looked after the family home, plus she worked and earned her own money. There was a big factory in Woking called James Walkers where I worked myself straight after I left school. I got a job working in the drawing office because being a draughtsman was what I thought I wanted to do at that time. I got an annual salary of £800 which eventually rose to £950. During my final months at school I had started an A-Level in Technical and Structural Drawing, but this was discarded after the first year of a two-year course because I got more into playing with The Jam.

Walkers factory seemed to have employed everyone in Woking at some time or another. They made rubber seals, gaskets and bath mats for the Royal Navy. John Weller, Paul's father, had a stint working there too. John had a variety of jobs, always changing, a brickie in the summer and driving taxi cabs in the winter, but back then there seemed to be plenty of work around. One time when John was working at Walkers he was told to go up onto the factory roof and do some repairs. Now because he was a bit of a Teddy boy he had the typical DA hairstyle, and tending to it was so important he always carried a comb and some Brylcreem. On that morning he had run out of Brylcreem so instead he put butter in it to achieve that slick-back look. Once he had finished the repairs on the roof he decided to stay up there for a bit longer and have a little nap. Unfortunately it was a hot summer's day and when he woke up all the butter had melted and started to go off so he smelt like popcorn.

That factory building had started off life as a college because of some links with Woking's Muslim community, and their mosque was the first in the country. Built in 1889 in Oriental Road, it was the result of the tireless efforts of an orientalist named Dr Gottlieb Wilhem Leitner. Having studied at madrassah schools that were attached to mosques in Istanbul, he moved to Great Britain at the age of 17 to study at King's College in London. In his mid-twenties he secured donations from Begum Shah Jahan, the Newhab Begum of the Princely State of Bhopal, and the UK's first mosque was built on the site of the Royal Dramatic College which served as a home for retired actors. In its early days there was a 'funeral Pyre' in the mosque to cater for the community's burial customs. The mosque also acted as a school where visiting dignitaries could live and study, and it flourishes to this day.

My parents had met before the Second World War broke out and came between them. When my dad returned from North Africa he went on a mission to reunite with my mum, restarting their relationship and, like a lot of people caught up in those times, strove for a better and more settled life. Both my parents worked hard and, looking back on the little we had, I never felt that we were missing out. There was absolutely no favouritism amongst us boys even though our ages were widely spread, and I have always admired them for treating all of us the same.

After John, Andrew was born, another boy! My mum got pregnant again and this time she had a little girl. Sadly the baby girl died after a few days. I think my mum then thought she'd give it one more go and try again for another girl. Instead twin boys, Peter and I, were born.

There was another twin connection in our family. My mum's brother, my uncle John, and his wife, my Aunt Margaret, had twin girls, Jean and Julie. They were born in June and Peter and I were born in December so being so close together in age we did a lot of hanging out. All of our Christmases and birthdays were spent in each other's company. Often Peter and I would be dressed in the same jumper and Jean and Julie would have the same dresses on; all Tweedledum and Tweedledee stuff.

Another aunt, my aunt Doris from my dad's side of the family, lived opposite our house. She was a right character, a proper old-fashioned card. She earned a living as a seamstress and so would make coats and other garments for other people. I remember that she actually made her own fur coat out of all the bits and pieces left over from her customers.

There were times when Doris would come over to ours, just to watch the TV. She would position herself right in front of the box and just sit there smoking her cigarettes from one of those long old-fashioned holders like you see in the black and white films from the thirties. Between the wars she had been a bit of a tearaway and she would hang out with the 'well-to-do' sorts from around Woking. She was well placed in the twenties and thirties to be going to posh parties where they did all those silly dances like the Charleston. Needless to say she had a bit of a reputation.

My mum always worked. She once worked in a shop in Woking called The Sports House. Oddly enough Bruce Foxton's mum also worked there. The shop sold tennis rackets, bows and arrows, cricket bats and sports clothing along with school uniforms. Then the supermarkets started to turn up and I remember early in 1971 my mum having to come to terms with decimalisation. Woking already had a Co-op in a big building, three or four storeys high, and at the top was a function room that could be hired for wedding receptions and other special occasions. Another large shop in Woking was Skeet & Jeffes on the Chobham Road, a hardware store painted in dull colours with dark and grubby worn out corridors. The showroom wasn't dissimilar to the layout in Grace Brothers... 'Are you going down sir?' It was all polite suited salesmen mixed with the strong smell of polished floor-wax.

My uncle John worked in Skeet & Jeffes after the war. The shop was really old fashioned and it fascinated me with all its tall shelves stacked with all sorts of hardware goods from hand tools to toilet and kitchen parts. I just didn't understand what most of these curious metal and rubber parts did and there were dusty boxes that looked like they hadn't been touched since the time they had been left there back in the days of Kitchener or something. It was also the place where all the local tradesmen would go to stock up on the parts that they required. My brother John told me recently that he recalls hearing his first swear words in that shop, from an impatient plumber.

Working in the shops meant mum wouldn't be at home on Saturdays, so dad would do the cooking at lunchtime. This usually meant we got fish fingers followed by Angel Delight, a real treat for us. Every other day mum usually made the dinners. We had fish on Fridays and a roast on Sundays. We didn't have a great deal of money so sometimes we would end up with some right ropey pieces of meat, the sort of meat we could only chew on rather than swallow. During that period sugar was still a real treat. If I could get away with it I would sprinkle as much as I could on my cornflakes. My mum would make the occasional sponge or fruitcake and we always looked forward to such home-cooked delights. A mother's cooking always seems the best.

My parents were Baptists and used to attend the local Baptist church in Percy Road. I would have to go too and actually enjoyed it, mostly because of the singing which Baptists tend to do a lot of. The first youth club I went to was held in an old shed next to the church and was run by church members. There was a boys club too but I never really got involved with that, though I did get involved with the Boys' Brigade. Sadly, there weren't enough of us to form a band. I think we only had one bugle to share between us. We did take part in some of the Boys' Brigades parades in the Surrey area, joining in with the larger Brigades and marching along behind them. It was good fun and the local community would turn out to lend their support.

Being involved with the church meant that we would also go off on our summer breaks with other members. One of the popular destinations was Swanage where the whole family would go camping. It was a good cheap holiday and near to the sea. The church would hire some huge marquees, which meant that they could serve as communal gathering areas for meal times. Then each family would have their own individual tents to sleep in. I did enjoy those holidays and I have a vivid memory of my dad trying to teach my mum to drive in one of the fields near to campsite. My dad had an old Ford Popular, a horrible car with only three gears. To add to the driving experience the field was on a good slope and the car would run downhill nicely and just slip on the way up on the long wet grass. My brother and I would just sit and watch from a safe distance, most entertaining. My mum never got the hang of it and never went out of her way again to learn to drive.

Back then it wasn't necessary to own a car, as it appears to be today. Certainly not everybody did and it would mostly be just one car per family. I remember the day my older brother got a car. That was quite an event for us. He managed to buy himself a smart looking Ford Anglia. We all stood around admiring it for ages. My dad learnt to drive because he worked for the Post Office telephones, usually in two man crews and sharing a red GPO Commer van.

My brother Peter and I spent a lot of time together when we were growing up. We went to the same schools and we would be in the same classes. Saturday afternoons would often be spent as a family day out, often with Jean and Julie in tow, sometimes an afternoon in the Lido at Guildford. There was a little boating pond, formal gardens and a big field that was perfect for playing in. Peter and I would also go to the Saturday morning pictures. I only remember two cinemas in Woking but I have been told that there were actually three at some point. I only remember the ABC and the Odeon. It was these two cinemas that presented the early Saturday kids shows. We would walk up there, on our own, for a 9.30 showing and for the next hour they would show Laurel & Hardy along with Captain Marvel and his magic word 'shazam' all in black and white; only some of the cartoons were in colour. We used to sit right down the front in the first few rows, until the manager got fed up with the amount of wet lolly sticks being flicked at the screen. We were all relegated to the back rows after that. If it was somebody's birthday the cinema staff would drag them out of the audience, up on the stage, give them a free lolly and everyone would sing happy birthday and clap. At the very least, going to the cinema did keep us out of parents' hair for a few hours.

If we weren't at the cinema we would play in Woking Park or on the Basingstoke canal. I don't remember there being any left-over bomb sites from the war, like there were in many towns across Britain. I don't know why the Germans spared Woking but they didn't drop many bombs on it. As a kid there were a lot of house clearances going on. There were whole streets of terrace houses disappearing. By the mid-sixties the planners (and their dreams) had well and truly moved into Woking.

A typical Saturday night was spent with the whole family huddled around the television watching the *Black & White Minstrel Show*. That was a big hit with my parents' generation. They loved all that singing and dancing. I sort of took an interest in *Dr Who* but it wasn't a big thing for me. I did however go to The Atlanta on Commercial Way to see a *Dr Who* exhibition. The organisers put up a big curtain across the room attempting to create some kind of 'other-worldly' effect. In the middle of the curtain there was a Tardis which we could walk into on one side and arrive in an area that had been decorated to represent the much bigger inside of the time travelling machine. And there were Daleks too but we could see the people inside them peddling them about; we were just kids but we were not fooled.

I really liked cartoons. There was always a slot on the television just before the six o'clock news where they showed *Tom & Jerry*. It was something I looked forward to because back then there weren't many TV channels, just BBC and ITV, and they didn't have many children's programmes. When I very young the radio was the big thing in our house. I suppose it must have been the same for most of my generation. Following our roast dinner on Sunday afternoons my parents often spent the rest of the day listening to *The Navy Lark* or *The Clitheroe Kid* or similar light-hearted programmes. They were mostly innocent comedy shows.

My parents would try to take it easy on Sunday afternoons. It was their rest time having spent the week working hard. My dad's hobby was making wooden model ships so he would steal some time to do that. He used to buy a magazine called *Hobbies* and in every issue there would be plans of how to make The Golden Hind or a famous steam train. It meant that if you stuck with it and depending on your skill you could end up with a replica of the HMS Victory or something similar. I still have one those ships that my dad made. I remember that he told me that he once started one of those ships before he went to war in 1939 and only finished it when he returned. He was a very patient man my dad, especially considering he brought up four boys.

CHAPTER TWO

Once I was five I started at Goldsworth Infants School on Goldsworth Road. Next door was the Goldsworth Primary School and next door to that was the secondary school, but I didn't get to go there as it was long gone by the time I was 11. It had been knocked down so instead I went to the newly built Sheerwater Comprehensive.

At Goldsworth Infants we were given small bottles of milk each day. It didn't last and I remember when the school stopped it. The school was quite progressive though, with its own tuck shop which meant I could buy Hula Hoops and bags of crisps with a small blue bag of salt inside to add and shake. There was no school uniform as such either. We were just required to adhere to some sort of dress code. The school buildings surrounded a little courtyard and in the middle of the courtyard there were two trees where we used to congregate during break times.

There was even an outdoor swimming pool, built while I was there, and I remember that they used us to help dig the hole and carry the buckets of soil away. Some of our sports lessons were spent labouring like this. The swimming pool had a small wooden fence surrounding it and the changing rooms were outside. They were more like sheds with partitions in them. The pool itself was always freezing cold. There was no heating whatsoever.

There were still a few air-raid shelters left dotted around Woking, and I recall playing inside some of them. They were more intriguing to explore than fun. They were just filthy disgusting damp holes in the ground with some half-rotting gas mask buried in one of the dark corners, but as kids we were left free to explore.

If we weren't breaking into old air-raid shelters we would go over to the shooting ground in Bisley. Looking back now this was extremely dangerous. We would literally be mucking around on the firing range, on our hands and knees, searching for bullet belts and bullet casings.

I got chased once. It scared the life out of me. I was rummaging around in some bushes trying to find stuff when suddenly this huge soldier appeared charging through the bushes towards me. I screamed, dived into the undergrowth and scurried away. He was too big to follow me so I escaped. But it did shake me up. The National Rifle Association (NRA) shooting ground at Bisley sprung up after it moved from its London home in Putney Heath and Wimbledon Common. I heard the story was that a stray bullet had killed somebody working in their garden. They uprooted everything, all the buildings and huts, and relocated to Bisley in 1890.

The Bisley Pavilion in the grounds of the NRA has for years hosted quarterly northern soul events called Nightshift, run by Derek Mead, but back then it was also a venue for live music. In the sixties and seventies it was very popular. I don't know why but The Jam never played there. We did however play at the Bisley Prison, Coldingley, on November 17, 1974.

My time at Goldsworth Infants seemed to flash by really and then I found myself moving up to the next level. It was an easy transition because I was still with Peter and all the kids from infants. It was while I was at Goldsworth Primary School that I became interested in sports, but then I suppose most kids are at that age. Kids like to play football and an assortment of team games. Generally speaking I wouldn't say that I didn't like school, but I wasn't in love with it either. School for me was just another one of those things that I took on board and just got on with. And during those primary school years I certainly didn't have any leanings towards history or maths or any of those types of subjects we were confronted with. No subject especially stood out.

I think the thing that I enjoyed above anything else was my friends. At that age it was about getting to know people. It was a time when I chose my mates and chose who I would hang around with after school. The majority of those mates were locals who I would see at the weekends anyway. But now I was at an age where I could hang out with them in my free time. It was different to my formative years, which had been all about hanging about with the family and not having a choice.

Every year the Post Office would run Christmas parties and they were tremendous fun. The Post Office where my dad worked had a big hall where some guy dressed up in a Father Christmas outfit and he would come round and give everybody presents. There would be food, lots of jelly and there would be lots of funny hats. It was a big event and something I really enjoyed every Christmas.

My dad, along with a lot of others from his generation, smoked cigarettes. Smoking was the norm and he would get into trouble when he lit up in the sorting office. Postmen weren't allowed to do that in case they set fire to the mail, but he was always sneaking a fag here and there though. Players Number Six was his brand of choice and they came with coupons that could be saved up and eventually swopped for something like a new teapot.

My dad didn't start driving until quite late which was a bit of a bind in some ways as it meant that we would have to pile into my uncle's Mini Estate. It was one of those designs with the wooden frames on the outside and was very cramped. The Mini would be jam-packed and we would go out and do something together for the day, perhaps drive to somewhere like Worthing. But it never seemed much of a day out because by the time we got to wherever we were going it was time to go back home. We mostly just had time to dip our feet in the sea and buy an ice cream.

But looking back most of the days out that I had with my family were spent in Woking Park where we would have a bit of a kick-about with a ball and maybe fly a kite. They had pitch and putt and even a lido, which was great fun to splash about in. Sadly the lido is now gone and the outdoor swimming pool was replaced with an indoor one. I'm not even sure the pitch and putt is still there any more either. In fact I'm not even sure the kids are even allowed to play ball games, such is the way things are nowadays. But when I was growing up it was very much a municipal park that was properly looked after and had beautiful landscaped gardens with rose bushes. It was always well attended and the gates would be closed at dusk and that was it for another day. It was all very civilised.

Sheerwater Comprehensive was a large mixed school, much bigger than Sheerwater Goldsworth which was tiny. I think Sheerwater must have had 1,500 kids whereas Goldsworth was just a few hundred. The kids that went to Sheerwater were also different from what I was used to. The whole of the Sheerwater estate was initially built as part of the Greater London Council (GLC) overspill, London having run out of land so they needed estates like this to house the growing population. The Sheerwater Estate was built as a result and in the middle of it they built the school and a small shopping centre. Many of the families that moved into the Sheerwater Estate were originally from London and the kids had a sort of street-cred that I wasn't familiar with.

The first couple of years at Sheerwater seemed uneventful really. Then a small group of us started to congregate in the rooms of the art department. We found the art teacher, Mr. Beach, quite inspiring and everyone called him Sandy. He was a brown belt in judo and a black belt Shotokan karate instructor. He had a big influence on his students and we felt that we benefited from his 'can-do' attitude. Such was his influence that I even joined the local karate club in West Byfleet. I spent many a Tuesday and Thursday evening and Sunday mornings there training and taking my grades with visiting Japanese examiners such as sensei Keinosuke Enoeda (1935-2003) and sensei Kato.

I think Sandy liked our little gang too and managed to secure some funding to purchase an 8mm movie camera and a small film stock. The aim was to make some short silent films, mostly of costumed fight scenes, with tomato sauce rubbed on us to create the blood effect. And they were filmed in the nearby Brookwood Cemetery and the Horsell Common sand pits, where the video for 'Funeral Pyre' was filmed.

My time at Sheerwater was a time of great introductions and music was one of them. It was the sixties and The Beatles were massive. I knew about The Beatles through my older brother Andrew. I have many recollections of Andrew bringing home records by bands such as Them and The Rolling Stones and he was a big fan of The Beatles. Andrew was a bit of a mod, always smartly dressed in a mod suit. And he always had nice looking girlfriends around him. The album *A Hard Day's Night* sticks in my memory because one Christmas, while me and Peter got a Scalextric kit, Andrew got a copy of *A Hard Day's Night* and played it constantly. We were very fond of that Scalextric kit as it was a shared present between Peter and me; all our Christmas presents were shared back then. But it was OK; after all there were two cars and two controllers so I suppose it made sense to my parents. On other occasions we would get a pair of bikes or identical jumpers – one with Paul knitted into it and the other with Peter.

Andrew was really my first introduction to popular music and then once I started to go to Sheerwater I started to bump into other kids who were also discovering music. It was the first time I noticed that some kids were into this genre of music or that genre. Around that time music really started to permeate me and my friend's lives. Looking back now – although it didn't seem that way at the time – I would find myself listening to music that my mates were into, while those that I wasn't particularly mates with I didn't listen to their music because I didn't need to. For example, during my time at Sheerwater I didn't really have any mates that were into David Bowie or Elton John. One of the things that struck me about Paul Weller when I first bumped into him was that he was into music that seemed to me to be retro. As a kid, if something happened to be a couple of years earlier, it seemed like years and years earlier. I remember Paul really liked Chuck Berry and he really, really liked The Beatles. What each of us listened to during that period made a massive impression on every one of us; at least that's how it seemed to me.

In those Sheerwater years there would also be a lot of album swopping going on. I would buy an album and listen to it and then swop with somebody else and get one of their albums in return. It was a cheaper way of getting through a lot of albums and getting to hear lots of different music. I remember conversations with my mates that were along the lines of, 'Look I'll buy this album coz I can't afford that album too, so you buy that album and we can swop after a couple of weeks,' and it kind of worked out. I also spent a lot of time around mates' houses listening to their records. Hours upon hours were spent digging around in someone else's record collection pulling out a variety of different albums.

At that time there were also albums called sampler albums, basically opportunities for record companies to showcase the bands on their label. These sampler albums were much cheaper than normal albums and often I would like two or three songs or bands on them. They did help to introduce me to new bands that I wouldn't perhaps have stumbled across. Looking back, those sampler albums were a good idea and inside the record sleeves there would be loads of advertisements about the bands featured on the album, a sort of 'and this band has also released these albums and…' As a result of one of those samplers I recall buying an album by a band called Iron Butterfly, but apart from the song that I had heard on the sampler I didn't like any of it.

The nearest youth club to where I lived was run by the local Percy Street Baptist Church. There were of course obvious rules like no drinking. Much of the music they played was dreadful. And they weren't particularly well attended either. Also, the people that went to them were the same ones that I had been going on holiday to Swanage with for years and went to the same church. I wasn't that thrilled.

Only once I started to go to Sheerwater did things start to change. By this time I was now hanging around with Paul Weller and Steve Brookes and before we went to a youth club we would buy a bottle of Scotch-Mac and drink it and then go to the youth club. This way we would be pissed by the time we went in. But there would be groups of kids standing in the corners trying to hide their miniature tins of Heineken and we would laugh at them as they would get caught and get thrown out.

Woking at the time just didn't seem that sussed really. I don't remember large numbers of skinheads roaming about, but I do remember a coffee shop in Bath Road where bikers would hang around. There were always big bikes and big guys wearing leather motorbike jackets. That coffee shop had one of those big coffee grinders rotating in the window and the smell that came out of that coffee shop was wonderful. I just don't think there were many places for kids to gather in Woking at the time. But there was another hangout, just around the corner in Commercial Way called the Atlanta. It had been an old music venue that in its hey-day had hosted performances from the likes of Johnny Kidd & The Pirates and Tom Jones. In the end the Atlanta was demolished to make way for a new shopping centre.

Most of my Saturday afternoons were spent hanging around different mates' houses listening to records and idling away the day. Peter would be around sometimes but it was around the time of going to Sheerwater that we started to drift apart really. We each started to make our own friends and have our first girlfriends, although at the time it seemed such a big leap to actually call them a girlfriend. In our own way we have always remained close though.

My whole social scene really got the kick-start around the time I attended Sheerwater. There were lots of people to meet and new things to discover. I would get invites to birthday parties or BBQs and because of this I would be bumping into new people and new girls. There was one party my mate arranged once he found out that his parents were going to be going away for the weekend. They went away on a Friday afternoon and as soon as they left me and my mate started to decorate the place with posters and all kinds of silly stuff. We put the invites out and word quickly got around. Inevitably the place got into a bit of a mess and then my mate's parents returned home earlier than they said they were going to. That resulted in a bit of scolding for us.

On the whole there just didn't seem much to do in Woking. So we had to make our own fun. There was another occasion when I, Paul Weller and Steve Brookes decided it would be a laugh to break into the building site down Commercial Way where some building works were going on for the new shops. We climbed up a ladder and were just larking around on a walkway. Suddenly Steve shouted 'Copper'. I looked around and saw this policeman running down the street towards us. The next thing Paul is rushing down the ladder closely followed by Steve. But by the time I got to the bottom of the ladder the policeman had hold of my collar and I wasn't going anywhere. Paul and Steve were nowhere to be seen. He took me to the police station and fired loads of questions at me. 'What you doing up there?' he asked. 'Well nothing,' I replied, which was true, we weren't really doing anything. Then he told me that they were sending a police officer back to the building site to see if we had done any damage and said that if there was any damage I was going to be in 'big shit'. And even though I hadn't done anything I was more scared in case my parents found out. After about two hours he just gave me a slap on the wrist and told me to bugger off.

I met Steve Brookes through Paul. At the time Steve was living with the Wellers and because of this arrangement he transferred to Sheerwater School. Those of us that were more interested in music rather than playing out in the yard during break times would go to the school's music rooms which the music teacher Mr Avery would allow us to use. There was a regular crowd of us that included Richard Flitney, who was a good guitarist, Nigel Constable, another drummer, Dave Waller, another guitarist and me, Paul and Steve.

There was also Howard Davies, a good mate of mine who played guitar who was in my first band, which was called Impulse. It seemed very important to at least have a name for the group. My brother Peter joined us on bass. We rehearsed at Howard's house, in the front room, and in fact we never got any further than rehearsing. We never played any gigs and it didn't amount to anything and after a while the band folded.

We played all sorts of rubbish in Impulse and because of that even started to call ourselves musicians. We weren't really, but me and Peter did have some piano lessons when we were younger. We had a piano in our front room at home. My mum couldn't play anything but my dad could play a little bit. Through the Baptist church connection we got to know a woman called Miss Jones and Peter and I had some piano lessons from her. Every Friday night she would come round to our house and give us a lesson, teaching us to play 'Hall Of The Mountain King' from Greig's *Peer Gynt* suite. Me and Peter would be perched side-by-side on the piano stool, our nostrils filled with the aroma of the cauliflower cheese that my mum would be preparing in the kitchen. Every music lesson night she made cauliflower cheese, which was Miss Jones' favourite meal. But I really hated learning to play the piano. I just couldn't take to it. The piano just didn't excite me one bit. Peter took to it much better and so by the time he came to play bass he had some degree of musical knowledge already.

However, I did take to playing the drums. I remember the Sheerwater School would occasionally hold music evenings and because they wanted somebody to play drums I got asked a couple of times. The school drum kit wasn't even a proper drum kit.

I don't really remember how or why I first got interested in playing the drums. I suppose when I listened to music I would analyse it and tune in to the drummers. To me the drums weren't academic. To play drums you didn't have to read music or understand musical notes. I just thought to play the drums all you need to do is just listen to the others in the band and just do it. But I needed a drum kit and the one subject I really enjoyed at school was woodwork. During those lessons I made a futuristic armchair. It was part of a project that we had to do. I made this armchair and it was quite big and my mum made the cushion which was one long stuffed cushion that ran its length. It stayed in the house for a while but never lasted because it was too big.

Our woodwork teacher, Mr Jones, encouraged me in those lessons and allowed me to make some drum shells. But because of the equipment in the workshop I had to make all the drum shells the same diameter. I ended up with a 14" snare, 14" tom and so on. But what I did do, however, was change the depth of each of the drums. Next I went to the music shop in Woking called Maxwell's, which mostly sold sheet music, trumpets and hired and repaired TV sets, and bought all the hardware (hoops and lugs) that I needed to complete the drums. I used to have to order the parts on a weekly basis from a catalogue and then it would get shipped in and I would pick it up.

By this time I also had a bass drum, which I had got from the Guildford YMCA where I used to hang around with my friends. I saw the caretaker there and he told me that if I took the drum home I could have it. So I picked it up and carried it away with me on the bus back to Woking. Once I got it back the first thing I did was spray it purple along with the other drums that I'd made. It was pretty dreadful really but it did work for a while and it did get me through the early learning period. Then I got hold of my first proper kit, a Hayman. It was a dark metallic blue, very nearly black. Again I had to buy the kit in instalments ordering bits week after week. One of my favourite drummers at that time was Paul Hammond, who played with Atomic Rooster, and he used a Hayman drum kit. I held on to that Hayman until I saved enough money to buy my first Premier kit in an Oyster finish, very similar to Ringo's.

I never had any drum lessons. I would just go and see bands and while there watch the drummers. Another local drummer that I knew obtained two tickets to see Buddy Rich and his band play at the Royal Albert Hall, an opportunity that I couldn't turn down. And even though I wasn't much of a fan of jazz music I knew that Buddy Rich's reputation as one of the world's best drummers was second to none. So we went to the Royal Albert Hall and thankfully we had really good seats that provided me with a great view of Buddy Rich. I just stared at him throughout the whole show. I focussed on him and watched everything he did. I simply tried to take in as much as I possibly could.

The venue was obviously packed full of drummers and you could sense that every eye was fixated on Buddy Rich. Halfway through one of the numbers Buddy stopped the band, got up from his kit, turned and demanded that the conga player behind him remove his shoes because he was tapping his feet out of time. The conga player did so without question. Suddenly, the Royal Albert Hall was filled with the sound of rustling as people in the audience were nervously slipping off their shoes. After witnessing what happened to the member of the band no one wanted to risk becoming the focus of Buddy's attention.

As a drummer I have always disliked setting up drums, then breaking them down, then storing them and having to carry all the cases around. I was very impressed with how Buddy Rich managed to utilise every part of his drum kit. He only had a small four-piece kit but he made it sound so huge. But I'm sure Buddy had needed to do his fair share of setting up and breaking down. But what he did, when he played, was so impressive. I was in awe of him.

Another important observation for me was noticing Buddy's curved posture when he stood up at the end of his performance. It was pointed out to me that his posture was crooked because he had spent so much time bent over his drum kit, and over many years of playing it had left him with a permanent crouched posture. I don't know if this was true but not wanting to end up like that I decided that I would always consciously try to maintain an upright position when playing. Thankfully it's a discipline I have always sustained.

CHAPTER THREE

Paul and Steve had already done some gigs at various working men's clubs around Woking. They mostly went out as a duo, but they sometimes used a local drummer called Neil 'Bomber' Harris. He was an already established drummer who played jazz and he preferred to wear a bow-tie when he played, which amused us. They had a gig arranged at the Sheerwater Youth Club that was run by Dave Strike. But Bomber couldn't make the gig because he was going away on holiday with his parents. Instead, Paul and Steve asked me to step in. At the time Paul and Steve were playing mostly Chuck Berry covers. I agreed, not really knowing what I was letting myself into, and was handed a pile of records to listen to and learn, and I had a week to do it in.

The Sheerwater Youth Club was more like an empty room where people used to meet up or just hang around. There never seemed to be much organisation. Mostly it was attended by kids from Sheerwater and was more of a place for keeping the local kids off the street. The hierarchy at Sheerwater meant we were careful of the year above us because they were the ones that were going to be trouble, bullies and so on. By the same token we felt we were superior to the kids below us. All these year differences seemed to be much bigger than what they actually were. That's a school experience we probably all share.

We made good friends in Sheerwater and many stuck by us as we developed as a band. Even many years after leaving school we would still bump into some of them. There was an occasion around 1980 that Paul, Bruce and I were in a hotel in Manchester and we saw a guy who we knew but we hadn't seen for years. For various reasons our lives had just gone separate ways. His name was Roger Pilling and he had been one of our original Sheerwater boys' gang. He had been to the gig and came by the hotel to say hello. He was a great guy who really stood out because he was tall and ginger.

We were all sitting around a table in the hotel chatting when from out of nowhere someone appeared waving a scrap of paper in front of us and asking if we would sign it for him. Of course we agreed and one after the other we all signed it, including Roger. We handed the piece of paper back and the fella walked away pleased. But he stopped a few feet away and studied his piece of paper. We watched as a puzzled expression appeared on his face. He then glanced in our direction before returning to his piece of paper. Then he tore off a corner of the paper and threw it to the floor. I guess he twigged that he had four signatures but there were only three members in The Jam.

By the time the Sheerwater youth club gig came around I pretty much had a proper drum kit and playing the drums was really starting to pick up momentum in my life. When I listened to music I concentrated on what the drummer was doing. I used to listen to the really good drummers but realised early on that I was never going be able to do what they did, at least straight off; they were doing some tremendous stuff. However, the records Paul gave me to study for the gig was all Chuck Berry and Jerry Lee Lewis and I could drum to them. It wasn't particularly hard drumming. The drummers that played on those records were more song based drummers, one of the things that I admired about Ringo Starr. Everything that Ringo did was confidently song based; he wasn't the type of drummer who played to outshine the band and prove himself as a drummer. Instead what he played fitted in with what The Beatles needed. It was a style and technique I decided to adopt. Plus it was my beginner's limitations that had driven me to these conclusions. So I learnt one 12-bar song and thought now I've done that I can play any 12-bar song... after all, all that changes is the lyrics anyway.

Leading up to the Sheerwater gig we had a couple of rough rehearsals in Paul's bedroom where we continued to rehearse for much longer. We got together and basically knocked through a handful of songs. I think at that gig we played 'Johnny B. Goode' and 'Long Tall Sally', among other well-known rock'n'roll standards.

The gig was absolute mayhem. We even had people jumping up on the stage. Paul was playing bass then, on a Hofner Violin bass similar to the one Paul McCartney played – indeed, Paul's real name is John but he wanted to be called Paul because of McCartney – and Steve played guitar. We hadn't worked out proper endings to most of the songs so they just carried on going until someone had had enough and yelled out stop. But we loved it, we had a cracking time. It was July 20, 1974, my very first gig playing with musicians in what would become The Jam.

There were no parents at the gig, none of the Wellers and certainly not my parents, although in Steve Brookes' book *Keeping The Flame* he remembers John Weller being present and giving the entire band a bollocking for being drunk. It wasn't that they weren't supportive; it's just that it really wasn't their scene. We were buzzing after the gig and that was why we decided to do some more together. Paul, Steve and I got together and worked out a proper set and we aimed for a more professional approach. We had loads of discussions back in Sheerwater music room and around Paul's house. We would throw in suggestions saying, 'We should do this one or that one.' We got very excited at the prospect of doing more gigs.

Gradually our set expanded and we managed to become more professional in our approach. Paul and Steve would tune up before we went on stage, and we would have set lists already prepared.

By this time John Weller was taking a keen interest in the band, although we didn't see Paul's mother so much. We would see Ann when we played the really local venues like the Woking Working Men's Club, which was just around the corner from where they lived in Stanley Road. John and Ann use to go there for an occasional night out anyway. Ann would make sure our shirts were ironed and that when we went out to play a show we looked clean, smart and tidy. I don't think Ann took it too seriously. I think she was the most sceptical because John's earlier idea of forming a youth football team for Paul had failed when it became apparent that Paul was the worst player in the team. However, as time went by John did get properly into what we were doing. He also liked the songs that we were playing because he liked fifties rock'n'roll. Even a lot of our school friends didn't really like what we were doing because what they were into was contemporary music like Elton John and David Bowie, and what we were playing was from a different era. But it was because we played the songs that we did that we got the work playing in the clubs around Woking. It was 'their' music from when 'they' were teenagers. They didn't want to hear 'Tie A Yellow Ribbon Round The Old Oak Tree'... but then never did we. Paul, Steve and I detested that song.

Our next step was to invite Dave Waller, a friend of Paul's, to join the band. I knew Dave from around school but Paul had been friends with him for a long time. Dave considered himself to be a bit of a revolutionary. He would try to blind us with quotations from Karl Marx but his heart was in the right place. Dave was brought in as the rhythm guitarist and Steve took on the role of lead guitarist. Paul would like to play tricks on Dave, on one occasion scratching the varnish off the back of Dave's guitar neck, which meant it was almost impossible for him to play and pretty much ruined the instrument as his hand kept sticking to the neck. Dave's Jedson Telecaster copy was his pride and joy. Playing with us wasn't for Dave and he eventually left; he just drifted away from the band. We all remained mates and there were no hard feelings.

John Weller took it on himself to look after us and was very much involved in finding us gigs in the very early days; nearly all only a short drive away from Woking, and mostly in the local working men's clubs. Through one of his contacts at Woking Football Club, we got a gig playing at Stamford Bridge, the home of Chelsea Football Club. I wouldn't have known a footballer if I fell over one, so the event was wasted on me. Football has never been of interest to me.

Additionally, Dave Waller's dad worked at the Woking Working Men's Club in Walton Road and this was how we secured regular work there. One set list from April 7, 1974 had 47 songs on it. To give some idea of the sort of songs we were doing the set list included 'Blue Suede Shoes', 'Blue Moon', 'Wooden Heart', 'Oh Carol', 'Save The Last Dance For Me', 'All I Have To Do Is Dream', 'Devil In Her Heart', 'Leaving On A Jet Plane', 'Slow Down' and 'Takin' My Love', then there was a well-deserved break before the second set where we continued with 'Proud Mary', 'More And More', 'When I'm Near You', 'Eight Days A Week', 'This Boy', 'Jailhouse Rock', 'Hippy Hippy Shake', 'Long Tall Sally', 'Three Little Words', 'Great Balls Of Fire', 'Whole Lotta Shakin'', 'Johnny B. Goode', 'I Saw Her Standing There', 'Twist And Shout', 'Little Queenie' and two songs held in reserve, should we get an encore: 'Crazy Old World' and 'Say Goodbye'.

The Conservative Club was a contender to become one of our regular haunts, but we turned out not to be the sort of thing the entertainment officer was expecting. John was very good at selling the band to these places and we did get asked back. The Conservative Club show was going well until the club secretary objected to Steve Brookes jumping up and dancing on the highly polished lid of the club's grand piano during the guitar solo in 'Johnny B. Goode'. Steve defiantly continued to play as one of the club officials tried in vain to get him off, chasing him from one side of the piano to the other. We just laughed and continued playing to the end of the song. The crowd looked on with bemused horror. Needless to say The Jam didn't get invited back.

I enjoyed those early shows and playing the type of venues that we did. We would play long sets with a short interval and they would often be in front of hard working and hard drinking people. The dressing rooms, if there were any, were mostly considered unnecessary or were nothing more than storage areas or toilets near the stage. Those toilets were basic but looking back compared pretty well to the dreadful toilets at the New York club CBGB where The Jam would play in 1977. Those toilets were something… unique… just like the club itself.

On one occasion, in one of the clubs we changed into our gear on stage behind a fire curtain, and it was the club policy to drop the curtain between acts. Unfortunately for us, someone decided to raise the curtain prematurely, which revealed us in various states of undress; shirts half on, trousers down and each of us hopping for cover. This, of course, provided an additional source of entertainment for the audience.

By now, we had decided on a stage uniform, thinking it would help us stand out from most of the other bands. There are several photographs floating around of us from that period wearing white satin bomber jackets, white kipper ties and white crepe shoes. This was a few years before we started wearing the black and white suits that were off the peg from Hepworth's, the tailors in Woking. It was a real stretch too. They cost a few quid and they didn't fit properly. Some of our outfits came from a small retailer called Daziels that offered items on the never-never. That shop is still in Woking but at the time it wasn't really a proper shop as such, it was run from a terraced house. This was a very popular way of shopping in the seventies. We would go into the front room and it would be filled from floor to ceiling with shoeboxes and jackets and shirts and trousers.

Following Dave Waller's departure we asked Bruce Foxton to join. We also knew Bruce from Sheerwater. Bruce didn't want to play with us at first and turned the offer down because he didn't like the music that we were playing, and he had his own band called Zita. But he did eventually join us, replacing Dave as the new rhythm guitarist. Something also needed to change as Paul was struggling with playing bass and singing; also, there had been an incident where Paul's beloved Hofner bass got sat on by Bruce in the back of the van after a gig. The guitars were laid on top of the other gear and were without proper cases. At the time Paul didn't see it as being the accident that it was and a fight broke out between him and Bruce. John Weller had to stop the van to calm things down. This was to be the first fight amongst Jam band members. I can still hear the crunching noise as the guitar neck came away from the body. It was repaired but it was never the same. A short while after, Paul said to Bruce, 'Right, you're going to play bass now and I'm going to go back to playing guitar.' It was a matter of either Bruce agreeing or leaving the band. Bruce agreed.

Paul opted to buy a Rickenbacker guitar, more for its cool looks than its sound, and Bruce started with another favourite of Paul McCartney's, a Rickenbacker bass. We were also introduced to the Dr. Feelgood album *Down By The Jetty* and Paul was especially influenced by Wilko Johnson's guitar technique. Wilko's style combined both lead and rhythm guitar in a unique way, a technique that Paul would also master and make his own, and it certainly contributed to the songs that The Jam would be remembered for.

With this new setup we felt like we had a proper band. By this time we had also settled on calling ourselves The Jam. The name only came about because once we started to play some proper shows we had to have a name. We decided on the name because we use to jam around together; so we said, 'Let's just call ourselves The Jam and if or when we think of something better we can change it.' We weren't really that enamoured with the name at all. We thought it was OK, would get us by and it would do until something else came up. We certainly never had any deep discussions about what we should be called. Many years later someone said to me, 'It's not the band's name that counts, it's the association with the band's music that counts.' They added that the band's name never makes a band a better band, which I suppose is true enough.

We would often get asked in interviews why we had chosen 'The Jam' as our band name and sometimes there would be a comment from writers along the lines of, 'Couldn't you have thought of anything better.' I remember that Paul was very envious of the name 'The Clash'. Paul thought that was a great name considering what was happening around that time. When we first started playing around Woking we didn't even know about the punk thing or the pub rock thing. We had very little idea what was going on in London. We didn't have a clue about any movements or scenes that were happening, we just had what we read about in the music press and that concentrated mainly on the big established acts of the day. The small gig ads at the back of those publications were often packed full of bands and venues we had never heard of, nor at first did we realise their future importance to us.

With Bruce now in the band we continued to rehearse often and we added more and more songs. For any band it's during those formative years when they really have to work hard at building a sound, an identity, and it was the same for us. Sometimes we all knew the songs anyway, so when we got together we would just play them and any bits that needed working out like a new chord that Paul, Steve or Bruce hadn't come across or an ending was then sorted out. Sometimes we would include medleys where we would just strap two or more songs together, and over time we got the hang of playing and rehearsing as a band. Mostly I just recall thinking verse, chorus, middle-eight, verse, chorus and end. We built up a good set that we pretty much stuck to night after night.

John Weller managed to secure us a regular Friday night engagement at a rather seedy nightclub in Woking called Michael's. The club was situated above a row of shops on the Goldsworth Road, accessed by a single blue door with a shuttered peep hole for security. It was one of those clubs that looked OK in the dark of the night but in daylight the décor was not so great. Things didn't really get going at Michael's until after about 10 o'clock; just before the local pubs were starting to ring their bells for last orders. Michael's was meant to be a member's only club, but virtually everyone was able to get in, as long as they wore a tie. In fact once you got to the top of the stairs there was a plastic bag full of ragged used ties that could hired from one of the bouncers. Joe Awome often took the job as security; a large good-looking semi-professional boxer who could be an intimidating figure and exhibit a strong presence, but in reality he was an easy-going giant. We all liked Joe and we became good friends with him. John Weller later employed Joe as one of The Jam's personal security.

Michael's was a home to all sorts of characters and was the scene of many incidents. One night an individual was refused admittance, probably because of previous bad behaviour, and later that night Pepi, usually the main man behind the bar, opened the small hatch in the club's front door to see who was banging so furiously. Suddenly there was a loud bang. The bloke who's been refused entry had returned with a shotgun and blown half of the door away. Pepi wasn't seriously injured but he did sustain some bruising and was found shaking under what remained of the door.

During one of our Sunday afternoon rehearsals in Michael's we had the session recorded. I don't recall how, but we came across a local chap who was a recording enthusiast. His hobby revolved around a reel-to-reel machine that he felt proud to possess. He wanted to exercise his skills in this area and offered to record one of our rehearsals. He set up a few microphones around Michael's and we banged out a live set. It went OK and we got some free recordings out of it. Rehearsing in Michael's was fun; especially as we used to try and help ourselves to whatever the bar had on offer. Most of the time this resulted in nothing though: the bottles of spirits were marked and closely watched.

There are rumours that a cassette is floating around of a recording from another rehearsal, this one at Woking Working Men's Club. It would be far from the best quality but does include some of Paul and Steve's early songs such as 'Takin' My Love', 'Some Kinda Loving', 'Little Girl Crying', 'Love Has Died', 'Love, Love, Loving', 'Like I Love You', 'You And The Summer' and 'Remember'. As you can see there was a great deal of love going around.

Michael's was also a great source of entertainment and certainly an education for us young boys on many levels. The shop below Michael's changed from time to time; it had been a nightclub, pole dancing club and a burger bar. At the back of the premises was a fire escape running from the top floor down to a loading yard. We would hang out there when we weren't playing or trying to blag a drink off someone. However, the main reason why we hung out there was because from that vantage point we could see the female dancers undressing in the changing room below. It would be a matter of creeping onto the fire escape and keeping quiet and still. We got caught out a few times but it was totally worth it.

By now John Weller had become our manager and our driver and generally took an interest in us and he looked out for us as a band. He was always borrowing vans from various people. There was one boy called Ronnie who John knew from Michael's. Ronnie owned a lioness cub but she had got too big to stay inside his house. One night Ronnie turned up at Michael's with what in the darkness of the club looked like a chunky dog on a lead. It was only when it growled that people realised what sort of an animal it was. People were both shocked and thrilled in equal measure.

Ronnie's lioness became a bit of a feature around Woking for a while because he used to take it for walks around the town. When it outgrew Ronnie's house he kept it in the back of a Luton box van instead. On a few occasions John managed to get Ronnie to transport our gear to and from gigs; the only thing was, wherever the van went the lioness went too. One time when we were returning home after a gig the lioness reached one of its paws through the partitioning window – we all used to travel in the front cab, well away from the lion – and rested it on John's shoulder. John, of course, froze as he nervously nudged Ronnie in the ribs. Ronnie responded by swiftly turning around and punching the lioness on its nose. She in turn retreated back into the darkness of the van and we all nervously laughed whilst sighing with relief.

When we borrowed the Luton and lion, someone usually opened the sliding shutter while someone else quickly pushed in the gear so the shutter could be closed as quickly as possible. After one show at the Tumble Down Dick in Farnborough a guy offered to help us carry a speaker cab back to the van via an old metal fire escape down to the car park. We hadn't mentioned the lion to him and he was totally unprepared when the shutter doors went up and he came face to face with a big cat leering at him. He promptly dropped what he was carrying and ran for the hills. A few months later some poor old woman wearing a fur coat attracted some unwanted approaches from the lioness and so it was sadly interned in a safari park somewhere.

On October 5, 1974 we had a show at Bunters Club in Guildford supporting The Rock Island Line, a Teddy boy band that was attracting a fair amount of attention off the back of the David Essex film *That'll Be The Day*. For a brief period, old-time rock'n'roll was back in vogue. It was a late club night and we were billed to go on before Rock Island Line. We arrived at the venue early evening, set up, did the soundcheck and then returned home so that we could have a wash and brush up and bite to eat. The only one who stayed in Guildford was Bruce. I think he had arranged to meet some friends.

On this occasion John had borrowed a different but equally dodgy old van that was difficult to get started. On the way back we had to stop and fill up the radiator with water from a nearby stream because a hose was leaking and the engine was over-heating. At that time in the early seventies the IRA was particularly active, and they had picked out two Guildford pubs, the Horse & Groom and the Seven Stars, to bomb. Guildford would have been in the sights of the IRA because the Pirbright Barracks were nearby and squaddies would venture into the town's pubs when they got the opportunity. The first of two six-pound gelignite bombs went off at 8.30pm in the Horse & Groom, causing five fatalities, two members of the Scots Guards, two members from the Women's Royal Army Corp and a 22-year-old man. A further 65 people were injured. The second bomb went off half an hour later, but thankfully there were no fatalities because the pub had been evacuated minutes earlier.

Due to the chaos and the emergency services rushing about on high alert we got a phone call from Bunters explaining what was unfolding around them and informing us that the show was off and we didn't need to return. We went back a few days later to collect our equipment and it was obvious that the town had been visibly shocked by what had happened in their community. It had also been a close shave for Bruce because he had actually been drinking in one of the pubs that got bombed, but had left with his friend a few minutes earlier.

That whole event got under my skin. Up until that point I only really thought of the IRA in terms of what was going on in Northern Ireland and in a handful of political hot beds, but it had all felt so detached. Those bombs in Guildford showed me that the Troubles really were now on our doorstep. This was also a few years before the Grand Hotel in Brighton got bombed, a hotel that The Jam would often stay in when we played at the Conference Centre. But Guildford was close to home; too close and my own personal awareness as to what was happening got heightened. The IRA and terrorism suddenly became very real for me.

A month after the Guildford episode we got a show via a local agent whose name was Wally Dent. We were booked to play the Coldingley Prison in Bisley on November 17 and included on the bill was a female solo folk singer and a band that played country & western, very Johnny Cash at Folsom Prison. The brave young woman attracted a great deal of heckling, but she must have expected some of that considering Coldingley was a prison for male lifers at the end of their sentence. But she held her own throughout her entire set, sitting comfortably and calmly on a tall stool. The audience was kept seated for the whole show as prison guards strolled up and down the aisles swinging their truncheons. Well, it wasn't that dramatic, but it was the seventies and prisons were no holiday camps back then. The reputation at Coldingley must have unnerved the drummer from the country & western band because he failed to show up. I was asked to step in and I foolishly agreed. I was given a red handkerchief to put around my neck in real cowboy fashion to add effect and I did my best, but not personally liking country & western music and not being familiar with the style of drumming, or the songs, it wasn't easy. I mostly just held down some sort of a beat until someone gave me a cue to stop. We got paid with government money, which appealed to us. It was worth doing and we gained a bit of local press in *The Woking News & Mail* along with a photo of Steve Brookes shaking hands with the governor outside the prison gates.

Around this time I was taking driving lessons and had just passed my driving test first time. The band was playing regularly and the money made from this was adding to what wages I was earning from doing various other jobs. Sometimes I worked extra evenings packing car baby seats for a company called Britax in New Haw, and in the day at their motorbike warehouse. They would store mostly consumables for motorbikes like exhaust pipes, brake pads and crash helmets. It was a good place to work apart from the practical jokes, usually at my expense. They would say to me, often just before lunch time, 'Oh we have an order for a part but it's right up there,' pointing to the highest shelf. Then they would drive over the forklift truck, I would hang on and they would forklift me up so I could hunt for the required part. As I rummaged around amongst the many boxes they would turn off the forklift and go for something to eat, leaving me up there until lunch time was almost over. I fell for that prank a few times.

I eventually managed to save up enough money to buy my first car – a second hand 850cc Mini. It cost me £25 and I bought it off a guy I had been working with at Herbert Machine Tools in Boundary Road. Having extra transport helped get the band to some gigs but things were put on hold for a short while following a bad car crash that I had. John and I were leaving London one night after having distributed some posters that advertised our upcoming shows. Bruce was also driving now and he and Paul were following us in his green Cortina. We were driving down the A3 and John had a plastic bucket with what was left of the wallpaper paste balanced between his legs. A lone candle in a council lantern was all that lit a railway sleeper that had been laid across one lane in front of some road works under a flyover. As this came into view I managed to swerve around it but a short distance on there was a second sleeper blocking the middle lane. Suddenly John grabbed the steering wheel, but unfortunately pulled us in the wrong direction. We ploughed into the sleeper causing the car to flip boot over bonnet before landing back on its wheels. The bucket seats that I had fitted a couple of weeks earlier were a help as they held us firmly in place as we rolled over. The bucket of wallpaper paste however span around the inside of the car and the paste had splashed everywhere.

Once John and I had collected our thoughts and quickly checked for injuries, an anxious John turned to me and said, 'My brains are coming out'. He wiped the thick paste from his face. He did, however, have a smallish cut on the top of his head from the caved-in roof but that was all. Once John realised that it was paste he sighed with relief. Within moments of the crash a very concerned Paul and Bruce rushed over to us. They had witnessed everything and naturally thought the worst. They sighed with relief once they realised that we were both OK. I did sustain a broken right foot and this made drumming a bit difficult for the next few weeks. I just played the next few shows with a plaster cast on my foot.

During those teenage years I had a few girlfriends but not too many. I only tended to meet girls once we started to play more shows in London. Because I was spending most weekends playing with the band I didn't get the chance to socialise in the same way as my mates were, and this meant they got to meet girls and I didn't. Having a car helped in this area and I did go out with a girl called Helen but she lived in south London. Having a car meant that I could drive from Woking to her home to see her. I was back and forth up and down that A3 like a violinist's elbow.

It can be a funny time when you leave school. Your circle of friends expands. Up until that point I only had my school friends, then I had people that I knew through playing with the band and then I had people that I was meeting through the different jobs that I was in. When I worked at the Walkers factory I got friendly with another crowd, then I worked for some electronics firm down Boundary Road and there was a bunch of girls who worked there on the line soldering components in printed circuit boards that I would meet up with again when I worked as an inspector at another electronics firm in Old Woking. So I met loads of girls but there were no real serious relationships during those years.

Throughout the early days of The Jam my drum kit mostly lived in Paul's bedroom. After each rehearsal or gig it would get stacked away in one of the corners. In fact at one time all of The Jam's equipment would get stacked up in Paul's bedroom. Only when we acquired bigger and more equipment did John Weller rent us a lock-up in an anonymous block of some very run-down garages attached to a block of flats. It was constantly damp and we had to stack everything up on palettes to protect the equipment from the puddles of water that collected every time it rained. Also there was no lighting and we hated having to drop the gear off in the dark after a show with only the van's headlights to see by.

I was never allowed to keep a drum kit at home, and so I could never practise at home. I really only learnt to play drums while rehearsing or playing gigs. Asking my mum if I could practise drums at home would have been like asking her if I could play football in the living room amongst the family china. But I would always carry a pair of drumsticks with me and I would practise on the end of my bed. I went through several bed sheets too, because over time the tips of the drum sticks would make holes in the sheets. My mum was forever complaining that one corner of the sheets was always torn and worn out.

Later, when we were no longer playing covers and writing more of our own material, I would draw on what I had heard other drummers play and think of signature fills or patterns for each song. Sometimes it was only small points that would help to make that song different in some way as far as the overall drum part was concerned. If I heard a particular pattern or fill, I would store it away in the back of my mind for later use. The sixteenths at the beginning of Deep Purple's 'Smoke On The Water' I had heard many years before and liked the way their drummer, Ian Paice, started the song. I incorporated the sixteenths idea into the pattern of 'Down In The Tube Station At Midnight'. This was not Deep Purple influencing The Jam but me scavenging from Ian Paice. I would do that with lots of songs, hear something I liked, file it away and tell myself that when the right song appears I'm going to use that.

Another example was a Steve Gibbons song where the drummer did a particular pattern and I liked that too; I found a use for it on 'Pretty Green'. So my use of drum patterns was my way of remembering what the song was and how it went. 'Funeral Pyre' was another song that was built around the drum pattern. The drums came first, acted as the foundation, then Bruce added the bass, then Paul came in with the guitar and lyrics. That was how 'Funeral Pyre' evolved but other songs such as 'Start' evolved because we took the idea from the feel of The Beatles' *Revolver* album. It wasn't just about 'Taxman' for us, it was more about the whole sound and feel of that album.

As I suspect is the case with most drummers, I always felt pressure not to keep playing the same pattern, which is what I had been doing while playing all those rock'n'roll songs in the early days. I would try to find space to add a little fill here and there and make it sound different to other songs; so something I would do on 'Running On The Spot' would be different to, say, 'Just Who Is The 5 O'Clock Hero'. As the drummer, this was something I felt that I could contribute to the songs. Take 'Pretty Green' for example, the whole song fits together rhythmically, it all pulls together. In 'Town Called Malice' there's a roll that I added because, for me, it was my way of trying to portray the sound of a train rattling along the track.

But all this came a few years into The Jam. The early years were very different. We worked hard at building a set. While we were doing this, most of the other kids on the Sheerwater estate were getting pissed in the Birch & Pines, a pub that had been built along with the rest of the estate. It was one of those hangouts where the 'younger lads' went, a place to be seen and to hang around the slightly older generation. It was that time that most people can relate to where it's cool to be seen with older kids, smoke fags and get served at the bar. For a lot of my school friends, to be part of the Birch & Pines crowd was a major aspiration because this was what their older brothers and sisters had done.

Not all, but many of my year at Sheerwater just wanted to leave school as soon as they could, get a trade such as plumbing or plastering and hang around the Birch & Pines. I didn't get so much time for this because being in a band meant that I was out playing most of the time, especially at the weekends. For me the band came first, and I think that Paul, Steve and Bruce felt this way too. We just didn't get the same amount of time to socialise or go to parties because we were working – not that we saw it as working – in the clubs. I would get invites to parties and events but the band was always the priority. I found that being in a band was exciting and provided a buzz on many levels. There weren't many people playing in bands so it kind of set me apart from others and I was happy establishing and developing my own individuality; playing in a band, playing in The Jam, even back then, felt special.

I was enjoying myself and we still found time to get drunk and fall about. There were many times when me, Paul and Steve would get drunk together and then it was a matter of trying not to go home too early, so as to try and avoid the parents. I would try and avoid going home until I knew they would have gone to bed. I don't think my parents ever busted me whilst staggering up the stairs. The other thing was that because I had started to play in the clubs from a very young age I had been around people drinking. And as a band we always found ways to get hold of alcohol.

Now that our name was about and we were playing the circuit, John was getting us bookings all over the place; night clubs, rugby clubs, football clubs, parties – anything really. We even entered ourselves into a talent contest held at the ABC Cinema in Woking. We got as far as the finals and found ourselves competing against an assortment of acts, only one of which was another band. We still didn't win. We also tried to get on *Opportunity Knocks*. The audition was in some big hall and all the acts were arranged around the edge. The judges moved along and stood in front of each act, tap-dancers, bands and soloists, giving them just enough time to impress them or otherwise. We played and they scribbled down some notes onto their clipboards and then we had to wait for the results. We didn't get anywhere but by the same token we weren't that gutted either. I think we knew from the moment we walked into that room that we didn't belong there.

Paul and Steve were now writing songs together, mostly Beatle-esque love songs. We had been gradually introducing the songs into the set and we decided it was time to try and record some of them. Bob Potter's small recording studio near his country club in Frimley wasn't too expensive to hire. It had one small drum booth, heavily padded, and a small control room separated by a main recording space. We were constantly reminded by the studio engineer that the monitor speakers in the control room had been used on The Tornados' hit record 'Telstar'. The drums on the recordings sounded really dead until loads of reverb were added.

For our first recording session we decided to do one of our own songs, 'Blueberry Rock'. During the few recordings in that period we would manage to get down four or five songs each session. I especially liked one song written by Steve and Paul that was called 'Forever And Always'. But these were all songs that were, in a sense, pre-Jam songs. What I mean is that once Steve left and after Paul had seen the Sex Pistols, his songwriting totally changed and so did The Jam. These early demo recordings were sent off to record labels like EMI and Decca but we got no response apart from a letter from Decca where they managed to spell Mr Weller wrong and inform us that what we had sent them was of no interest to them whatsoever.

One day John announced that he had got us a show supporting a band called Thin Lizzy at the Greyhound in Croydon. It was Sunday, October 27, 1975, and if memory serves me right I think the band were going to get paid £5 and we were told that we would get the opportunity to play in front of 1,500 people. We had heard of Thin Lizzy because they had already had a hit with 'Whisky In The Jar'. The show we would be supporting them at was part of the tour they were on to promote their new album *Jailbreak*, which included their next big hit 'The Boys Are Back In Town'. As a band we were still wearing the white satin bomber jackets and kipper ties. Loads of bands in the seventies had their own distinct uniforms; The Bay City Rollers with their tartan and our white satin bomber jackets. But our look didn't go down particularly well with the Thin Lizzy crowd, and to add to our discomfort the Thin Lizzy crew refused to mic us up. We were allowed to use the vocal mics but nothing more; so my drums were not amplified which meant I had to bash them really hard. Our sound was shit and we went down really badly; plus we looked ridiculous and played all these old rock'n'roll numbers. We really didn't appeal to that early Thin Lizzy crowd of long hair and denim. What's more I'm not sure we ever got our money for the show.

Nevertheless, that Thin Lizzy show was a good experience for us. It was a whole new world that we knew we had to try and get into. We also knew we had to somehow break into the London circuit. The band was moving on and we were discovering new things, new records and getting better at playing together as a band. We had been offered a couple of decent shows supporting bands like Stackridge, also at Croydon, and playing at prisons and football clubs and these were prestigious gigs as far as we were concerned. But a few things happened that I think contributed to Steve Brookes wanting to leave. The last straw incident happened when he was carrying a big speaker cabinet up some stairs and he bashed his thumb on the hand rail. I think he was already getting a bit disillusioned, because despite our playing plenty of shows we weren't making lots of money. We were well established on the club circuit in and around Woking but we were sort of in a rut and just going round and round, in a circle, playing the same venues to the same faces. It didn't feel like we were getting anywhere. And so

Steve just decided he'd had enough and said, 'Right I'm off' and he went and did his own thing as a solo artist.

Now one of the most difficult things for any band is to try and stay together. It's important for all the members to have the same vision with everyone pulling in the same direction. We still felt that if we were going to be a proper band we would need to have four people in the line-up. All the best bands that we took our influences from, like The Beatles and Kinks and Small Faces, all had four members. So in an attempt to replace Steve we held some auditions at the Red House in Woking.

We auditioned several guitarists, including Brian Viner with whom I became good friends, but none of them were right for us. We even auditioned a keyboard player whose name was Bob Gray. Bob played a couple of gigs with us; one of these supporting the Sex Pistols in Dunstable. But still, having a keyboard player in the band didn't seem to fit in with where we going musically by that time. As a unit, Paul, Bruce and I were at a point where we were really gelling together, just the three of us.

We also realised that sending demos into record labels wasn't getting us anywhere. We realised that we needed to be playing shows in London to have any chance of getting spotted by the record labels' A&R men. This was a time when the London pub rock scene was really happening. I would avidly read the music papers and keep an eye on who was playing at the Rochester, the Red Cow, Nashville Rooms or the Hope & Anchor and so on. I knew that's where we needed to be.

I was in my late teens and still listening to the music that I had always been listening to. The more I got into drumming, the more I would buy records because I liked the drummer. Paul Hammond (Atomic Rooster and Hard Stuff) was a big influence on me as I was learning and absorbing all I could. A lot of the big rock acts, like Deep Purple and Led Zeppelin, were beginning to become 'not' the thing to listen to. Instead, I was becoming more aware of bands such as Kilburn & The High Roads and Dr. Feelgood. These were bands that the music industry and the majority of the general public didn't regard as *Top Of The Pops* material. The 'sweet part of the pie', bands like The Bay City Rollers and The Three Degrees, performed on *TOTP*, but the pub rockers playing in London certainly didn't.

The music outside of mainstream radio and TV was very much 'more real' to us, and I knew that my friends felt the same way. There was also a hunger to escape and not just with music or drugs. There was a bit of a drug culture going on around Sheerwater, some guys getting hold of speed and a bit of heroin, but mostly just puff.

We would often head up to the Lyceum in London. The shows didn't start until 11 o'clock and then ran until six in the morning. A crowd of us from Woking that often included me, Dave Waller and Paul Weller would travel up on the train. It was at one of these Lyceum shows that Paul saw the Sex Pistols and this really changed his mind about everything. They made a huge impression on him. Up until that point, most of the bands that we were seeing at the Lyceum were older than us, a sort of generation before us, but the Sex Pistols stood out because they were the same age as us. Also for Paul, discovering the Feelgoods and realising that a band could play as a three-piece, with the guitarist playing rhythm and lead at the same time, was a massive revelation. From this point on The Jam changed.

I saw lots of bands at the Lyceum, including a Welsh group called Man, but most were simply a backdrop to the night itself, though I used to keep a scrapbook of all the bands that I saw which I still have. They certainly weren't the bands that you would find on *TOTP*, but seeing the bands was only part of the night out, with drinking and having fun with my mates the real reason for going. It was a really exciting time in London; a proper buzz. This was my first indulgence in some kind of scene; somewhere between pub rock and punk and the remains of an old hippie happening. We did come across The 101ers once, and this was because The Jam was booked to play at the same venue as them. I think it was at the Hope & Anchor. Once we turned up and the promoter told us that we had to go home, explaining that The 101ers had been booked to play instead. Back then there were so many bands wanting to play that the promoters could book two bands on the basis that if one band didn't turn up the other could play and this way the venue would always have a band. Some of these promoters thought nothing of telling a band to fuck off once they arrived, no matter how far they had come.

Although we were pissed off that we couldn't play, we reloaded our gear back into the van but we did stay to hear The 101ers' soundcheck. I remember having a conversation with Joe Strummer but at the time he was just another musician from another band, and one who had nicked our slot too. The next time I saw Joe Strummer was at Soho Market when The Jam set up our gear and played a few songs in the street. Joe and two other members from The Clash, Mick Jones and Paul Simonon, ambled down to see us play. We thought that by doing the Soho thing it would achieve either one of two things: we would get mentioned in the music press or we would get arrested.

Thankfully, we did get a small mention in which journalist John Ingham on October 23, 1976, wrote: 'With bands far exceeding the number of London clubs sometimes you really have to take it to the streets. Last Saturday The Jam did just that. Setting up on the pavement outside Soho Market about 12.30, they ripped it up for almost an hour. A small appreciative crowd developed, complete with beggar. The firemen at the nearby station watched from the roof. The Clash enjoyed their breakfast to the rocking strains. Natives of deepest Surrey, The Jam looked as though they had just been released from school, though their black suits, white shirt, black tie combination could be to invoke the mid-sixties. Beat Boom correctness. Guitarist Paul Weller must be the quietest guitarist in rock, quite Wilko Johnson influenced, but capable of providing some real excitement. The rhythm section (Rick Buckler drums and Bruce Foxton bass) was solid, but could use less cabaret. Their songs also invoke mid-sixties beat boom and could do with a bit more musical originality. There're some good things in there,

Rick in 1982. NILS JORGENSEN/REX FEATURES

My mum and dad with my oldest brother John in the sixties. RICK BUCKLER ARCHIVES

School friends, Tony Pilott (RIP), Dave Waller (RIP) the original rhythm guitarist and Rick. RICK BUCKLER ARCHIVES

Once we tried to rehearse in Paul's back garden one hot summer day in Stanley Road but the Police were called because of the noise.
RICK BUCKLER ARCHIVES

Back door of the Weller house in Stanley Road.
RICK BUCKLER ARCHIVES

Rick's first band Impulse formed with his brother Peter and school friend Howard, rehearsing in the front room.
RICK BUCKLER ARCHIVES

The Jam as a four piece at The Winning Post, Twickenham, Policeman's Ball. RICK BUCKLER ARCHIVES

We were sometimes introduced as 'Hey Man The Jam'. RICK BUCKLER ARCHIVES

Lesley and I first met in 1977 and our first date was when I got rid of my dark green Austin 1100 and bought a red TR6.
RICK BUCKLER ARCHIVES

Just off stage after a good show at The Greyhound, London, 1976. RICK BUCKLER ARCHIVES

Portsmouth Guildhall, May 24, 1979. Drum technician Ian Harvey is behind the bass stack. DENIS O'REGAN/CORBIS

Hammersmith Odeon, 1977. IAN DICKSON/REX FEATURES

The video shoot for 'News Of The World', on top of Battersea Power Station. TONY NUTLEY/REX FEATURES

Rick on the tour bus. RICK BUCKLER ARCHIVES

especially In The City I've A Thousand Things I Want To Tell You. The sun shone, no police came by and the last three songs were hot stuff. Judge for yourself, November 9, at the 100 Club.'

CHAPTER FOUR

After the Soho Market busking adventure we went back to Woking and picked up where we had left off, continuing with the club and pub gigs. What the Soho thing did do was give us all more of an appetite to get more involved with what was going on in London. We had seen The Clash and Pistols and we saw what they had and saw that it was something that we wanted to move into.   This was 1976 and we had been playing for a few years and felt that we had served our apprenticeship. We knew playing London wasn't going to be financially beneficial, even compared to the meagre wages that the provincial clubs were offering, and we understood that the gigs wouldn't be as consistent and that we'd have to take what we could get. What we also understood was that there was a lot of competition with other bands to get gigs. John Weller worked really hard to get us gigs during that time. The competition was fierce too, because there were already lots of well-established bands playing the London circuit. John had to justify to the venues that The Jam could pull in and hold a crowd.

So we were between two places; still doing rock'n'roll covers but wanting to appeal to the punk scene. But we didn't see ourselves as being part of the punk thing; although we had much in common with the ideals or sentiments of what we had come across, we simply saw it as us getting in on what was happening in the London pub rock scene. I think, as far as Paul was concerned, he suddenly realised that he could really have a direction with the content of his songs; and his songs had literally changed overnight ever since he had seen the Pistols and we had discovered an audience of our own age. It went really quickly from songs such as 'Lovin' By Letters' to songs that had real content. It was exciting to do something more than ballads and love songs. We did have 'Takin' My Love' and we did play it a bit harder, but a song like that had drawn inspiration from blues and rock'n'roll anyway. The influence was no different to The Rolling Stones breaking new ground, but musically they were basing their songs on blues and rock'n'roll too.

I think the thing I found most exciting about starting to play the London gigs was that we were now playing to people of our own age. Previously, we had been playing to punters in pubs and clubs that knew and remembered the cover songs we did from when those songs first came out. It was familiar and it was comfortable for them. I think Paul got a lot out of writing songs that related to our own generation and now he could write songs that were looking forward rather than backwards.

Suddenly, because of what was going on in London, record companies were sniffing around. At this point none of the punk bands were signed but the feeling was that it was only a matter of time, and we were all wondering who would be the first. Chiswick Records approached us and offered us a deal. The deal wasn't great; it was something like £600 and the free use of a PA system. Paul, Bruce, John and I discussed the offer and decided to turn it down. We felt that there were going be other offers and we had heard from some of the other bands that some of the bigger record companies such as EMI, CBS and Polydor were on the hunt to sign punk bands.

There was a big buzz around, a lot of expectation and people were asking which punk band would be the first to get a record released. As it happened, The Damned beat everyone else to it when Stiff

Records released 'New Rose' on October 22, 1976. I remember thinking at the time, 'What a great recording'. Even at this point I hadn't even seen The Damned as whenever they were doing a gig, so were The Jam. There were many bands I would have liked to have seen around this period, but couldn't for the same reason. I would usually only get to hear about what the other punk bands were doing after talking to the fans at Jam gigs.

So 'New Rose' was out and punk was starting to grab some media attention; so much happened in such a short period of time and within the space of three or four months everything changed. By the end of 1976 The Jam were securing London gigs at venues like the Roxy, the Nashville Rooms and the Red Cow. We also had a gig supporting the Sex Pistols at the Queensway Hall, Dunstable, on October 21. This was a warm-up prior to advertised shows and the release of their debut single 'Anarchy In The UK' which was released in November. The Pistols hadn't long been signed to EMI, The Damned had Stiff Records and we were still waiting.

We got the call the night before asking us to be the support act, and since we hardly ever turned anything down we drove to Dunstable with a fourth member, our piano/keyboard player, Bob Gray. At this time we were still convinced that The Jam needed to be a four-piece, even though we were always struggling to stay as a four-piece. I think we had only one rehearsal with Bob, then went to Dunstable and played our usual mix of rock'n'roll and R&B classics, with a handful of our own songs thrown in. It was a very disappointing crowd, only a few people scattered around the hall; I think I counted only about 12. The Dunstable show was very low profile because it was intentionally poorly advertised. If it had been after the Grundy show it would probably have been jam-packed.

What I do recall from that show, as we left the stage, was feeling a bit deflated because there hadn't been many people to play to. But what impressed me was that when the Sex Pistols went on they pulled all the stops out. It seemed to make no difference to them that there weren't many people there. The Pistols went out onto that stage and played really, really well. I learnt from that, it showed me that this is what a band has to do; it shouldn't matter if there are only a few people in front of you. And the Sex Pistols sounded good. All the stuff I had read in the media about them not being able to play wasn't what I witnessed. I was surprised by the sound of Johnny Rotten's voice and he was so entertaining to watch, there was something so magnetic about him. The band was good too, they were a good rock band, and it was great to have seen them at that time.

Bob Gray didn't last long in The Jam. I just don't think he was interested in the punk thing, so we ended up back as a three-piece. We always seemed to gravitate back to being a trio and after Bob left The Jam really became that permanent three-piece that would carry us through for the rest of our time together.

Soon after the Dunstable gig there was the Bill Grundy incident. The *Today* show was broadcast on Granada TV at 6pm on December 1, 1976; live and uncensored. The Sex Pistols had been invited in to replace Queen, who had pulled out at the last minute. I didn't see the programme at the time but certainly saw the aftermath. Some people were generally outraged with the Sex Pistols' behaviour, but many of my generation didn't have a great deal of love for the Bill Grundys of the world, so they reacted differently. Bill Grundy represented the old guard, the establishment.

What the Bill Grundy show did was bring punk to the attention of the nation, but as far as I and those I knew who also played in bands were concerned, the whole punk thing had exploded several months earlier. The Roxy had been regarded as the main centre where hard-core punks gathered. It was at the Roxy where you'd see people wearing bin-bags and safety-pins hanging off their shirts and trousers. It was a scene where people were trying to be different but then, after the Grundy show, punk left London and everyone became different by 'being the same'; that's what happens with those sort of fashion movements, they get injected into the mainstream very quickly and are then no longer what they were like in the beginning.

I remember taking a trip with Paul down the Kings Road and seeing Malcolm McLaren's shop SEX but we didn't go inside. Instead, we went to the shop next door called Johnsons because they sold striped boating jackets and this was a look that The Jam was getting into; this was about 18 months after the Bill Grundy show. I think SEX closed in 1976. The stuff that was sold in SEX was a bit too extreme for us; all bondage and fetish gear and much too strange for us in The Jam and even most of the punk fans.

The years 1976 and '77 were a good time for music and I thought The Damned's 'New Rose' was great, the way it just thundered in. It was a great song that seemed to burst with energy every time I played it. I loved the way it starts with the drums and then, bang, it's straight in there. 'New Rose' was a sort of flagship song for the whole new movement. Also, because all the press was banging on about the punk scene in London, 'New Rose' sort of broke out and cleared the way for us. There was suddenly a buzz around and we wondered who and what was going to be the next punk song to be released. 'New Rose' and the Grundy show did all of us other bands a favour too, because after them we all found ourselves being booked to play national tours. Then there was the opportunity to follow up singles with albums too.

I know The Clash refer to the importance of The Ramones' first album and once we looked past our own back gardens I also discovered other bands like The Ramones. There was something exciting about that sort of high energy music. I didn't see The Ramones as being a punk band like us, they were a punk band, but an American punk band and what they had was different to what was happening in Britain. To me The Ramones were like high energy Motown. They did the fast 1-2-3-4 count, then into a three-minute song and that was a very British thing. It's that sort of cut to the chase thing and I could relate to that.

Plus there was also the Malcolm McLaren connection. He had been to America and been involved with The New York Dolls so he had a handle on what was going on in clubs like CBGB, and he brought those ideas back to the UK. McLaren had a great talent for being able to make things happen; it was McLaren that supplied the machinery and provided the base for the Pistols. He had the spark that was needed to ignite the punk explosion.

I think what McLaren did was fabulous. It helped all of us bands, from The Lurkers to The Clash. Strummer had been in The 101ers, which had been a pub rock band but then Strummer evolved into what he saw was the new scene. I think in some ways this was what The Jam did too. It's hard to imagine what would have happened to Paul's songwriting if there wasn't a punk scene.

Another thing was that people became interested in the ropey old black and white suits that we were wearing, and there was a certain amount of kudos about them. That period felt like everything was starting to fall into place and it felt to me like we had adjusted and become part of the London scene, which is what we had wanted to do. We had the beginnings of a new audience. I remember Shane MacGowan would show up all the time. I have photographs of Shane standing in front of The Jam at the Nashville. He was one of our earliest hard-core fans that would follow us around. Then he went on to form his first band, The Nipple Erectors. I still have their single. They soon shortened their name to The Nips.

It was at one of the gigs in the Nashville, early '77, that Chris Parry came to see us. After the show he came back to the dressing room and made himself known to us. He introduced himself as an A&R man for Polydor and said that he liked what he heard and was going to talk to his superiors about us because he wanted to secure us some studio time so that we could record some demos. We listened and we were interested but we were still sceptical; we had heard it all before. Plus there was some rumour that CBS were hanging around our shows and The Clash's shows too. There had been an occasion a year or two before when someone had approached John saying they could get The Jam a tour in Europe, supposedly doing the rounds of American Air Force bases in Germany. I was working at the James Walker factory at the time, in the drawing office, and even handed in my notice, but then the tour came to nothing, so we took these things with a pinch of salt.

However, Chris did return for another show, and told us that he had booked us into Anemone Studios, the first proper recording studio that we had been into. We recorded a handful of songs to be used as demos. Chris said he was pleased with them and thankful that we could actually record in a studio, and he took the tapes to the 'powers that be' at Polydor. We had to sit back and wait for a couple of weeks for their response. Then John phoned me at home. I remember my dad answered, and called me to the phone in the kitchen – because he worked for Post Office telephones, he had installed an extra telephone, very unusual at that time – and John told me that Polydor had been in touch and that they wanted to sign us for a single. I was thinking, 'This is fabulous' but I couldn't quite believe it. I suspect Paul and Bruce felt the same way.

None of us really had an idea if the Polydor deal was even any good. All we knew was that Polydor was a bigger record company than, say, Chiswick; but they were still only offering a one-single deal with a possible option for an album. But we also knew that we wanted to be up there along with The Damned, The Clash and the Pistols, so we decided to do it. And then once we had made that decision we all got very excited.

We went down to the Polydor offices, which were in some unassuming tower block. It didn't look impressive at all. We stepped out of the lift at what was the top floor and we were met by a more lavishly decorated entrance and there were gold albums and single discs with the company logo hanging proudly on the walls that surrounded the reception area. I remember noticing discs by Slade and feeling quite in awe.

Chris Parry came out of an office to greet us and we followed him into one of the other offices. He did his best to explain to us the deal in layman's terms; what was on offer and what we needed to do. Included was the recommendation, if not a demand, that a professional manager be appointed to replace John. Their reasoning was that they thought the band needed someone with more experience and who also understood the industry better. Names like Brian Morrison, along with others who Polydor already worked with, were bandied around. They basically said to John, 'You've done a good job but now this is for real.'

We hadn't expected the 'new manager' recommendation and our immediate and unanimous response was that we weren't going to sign the contract without John being on board. Paul, Bruce and I had absolutely no intention of signing a deal that would result in John, who had looked after The Jam very well for the past few years, getting sidelined. Looking back now, I think Polydor presumed that our reaction would be to defend John and they quickly changed their tune, saying, 'Well, if that's the situation, John can remain as your manager but he'll have to take advice from the professionals such as the booking agents, the solicitors, the publishers and the accountants.' John wisely agreed to take their advice and be guided by the agent and publishers appointed by the record company. They also made it clear that they were on our side, which they were; after all, they wanted to ensure that the records would sell. So we left that meeting a step closer to signing with Polydor Records and went back to the Princess pub in Maybury to celebrate in our usual fashion.

A few days later we returned to the Polydor offices for another meeting. Only this time we were ushered into a much bigger room with a much longer desk. And it was during this meeting that we actually signed the contract with Polydor. Again there was plenty of advice being thrown at us. We had people trying to tell us that we needed to make sure we look after our money properly and we all understood the terms of the partnership that had been set up, not just with Polydor, but also between the three members of The Jam and John Weller.

From this point on everything seem to move really fast. 'In The City' was identified very quickly as the single and 'Takin' My Love' was agreed upon to serve as the B-side. Polydor believed that 'In The City' was the song that was best suited to introduce the band to the public en masse. Paul, Bruce and myself were happy with the decision, after all it was one of our newer songs and we felt it described who we were and what we were doing and it reminded us that we were moving out of Woking and seriously breaking into the London scene and beyond. It gave us a tremendous buzz.

Polydor booked us into its in-house recording studio which was in Stratford Place, just off Oxford Street. Chris was genuinely behind the band and he gave us every support in the studio. He introduced us to the in-house engineer Pete Wilson. They both saw the anthem-like potential for 'In The City'. Chris also acted as co-producer. On the day of the recording Paul, Bruce and myself all turned up at the same time. I dragged my black Hayman kit along and Paul and Bruce their Rickenbackers.

The actual recording was easy because we already had some recording experience and were well rehearsed. We played the songs live and then did overdubs. As a team we worked quickly. We were used to that too, because we understood that recording sessions cost a lot of money.

'Takin' My Love' was a song that went back to the days of the songwriting partnership between Paul and Steve Brookes, but it was also a song that was very much a collaboration between all the band members. At the time it wasn't an issue at all. And certainly back in 1977 I had no understanding of the gravitas of the implications of whether my name was on the publishing contract or not. I didn't consider the consequences of such a thing. I doubt any of us did. I was just excited that we were finally going to get a record out and that it was going to be a national release.

In addition to the release commitment from Polydor we had a £6,000 advance which, although they controlled how to spend it, still meant a great deal to us. So I was just going to enjoy it. After all, for all we knew it could have only lasted six months and before long we could have found ourselves back working in a factory in Woking with The Jam playing Michael's again. We just didn't know what the future would hold for us, the only thing that seemed to matter was that we stuck together with a common goal, in the same way we had always done. We all knew we could not have got this far without each other's support.

The fact that we only got an advance of £6,000 but The Clash got £100,000 from CBS – according to punk fanzine *Sniffin' Glue* that was 'the day punk sold out' – just didn't matter to us. Besides, it wasn't like we each got a wad of cash to blow. The Jam's advance was pretty much allocated for us by Polydor, that's what record labels do, they are very skilled at spending bands' monies on the bands' behalf. The Jam's advance went on studio time, paying the accountants, paying the solicitors – which paid for the very contract that had been negotiated – and we didn't see a single penny. In fact, years later there was at one point a very large deal on the table and I didn't see much of that either except for living expenses or the odd small payout after a tour. Instead, it went on paying for the recording of the album, tour support, transport, crew wages and settling hotel bills and taxes.

Once 'In The City' was recorded we were introduced to Bill Smith who was to design the single sleeve. In those days most records that were released had covers that brandished the record label's company logo, but there was a growing trend to return to the glossier packaging of picture bags that had been fashionable in the sixties.

For our first proper Polydor photo shoot we dressed in our black suits and white shirts and were marched outside and around the corner to an alley and directed to stand against a wall. The words The Jam were hurriedly sprayed on the wall, by Bill, in a graffiti street style of writing. This version of The Jam with the M underlined cemented itself as the official Jam logo. There wasn't a lot of pre-thought put into it; it seemed very spontaneous. It was the first logo we had had since I had designed one back in the mid-seventies. There is a photograph of that logo that I designed (and it's very prog-rock) of me, Paul and Steve Brookes on stage at Michael's. Recently someone found the photograph while sorting through photographs at a boot fair. They got in touch with Dizzy at Detour Records and he forwarded the photograph to me. In that photo the logo is painted on my bass drum skin; it just says Jam not The Jam. This was something I never did again. I wasn't against having the band's logo on my bass drum; it was just one of those things that I never thought about. The other thing is The Jam from 1977 onwards always went for backdrops anyway, so everyone could see who we were.

There was quite a buzz as the release date for 'In The City' approached. Polydor informed us that the pre-sales figures were looking good and they hinted that it was likely that an album could follow. 'In The City' was finally released on April 29, 1977. We had been doing shows constantly throughout February and March leading up to the single's release. We had been playing all over London, two shows at the Roxy, several at the Red Cow, more at the 100 Club, the Marquee, the Rochester, the Greyhound and the Hope & Anchor.

We had also played our first show outside of the UK, the Palais Des Glace Punk Festival in France. The word of what was happening in London was obviously spreading. We returned to France in August for the Mont De Marsan Punk Rock Festival; only this time we didn't get to play. We arrived a day early and spent some time hanging around, taking in some of the emerging bands and local sites. The turnout at the festival was a curious mix of festival goers, hippies and bikers and then there were a few French punks (who had learnt how to dress in a punk style from the London press). I made a beeline for The Damned's afternoon set. When Rat Scabies entered the stage he tried to stand on his drum stool, he was evidently pissed and after a few attempts and much wobbling, he gave up and just got on with playing the set.

Instead of hanging around the festival Paul and Bruce had gone into the nearby town. They got drunk and were arrested and detained by the local gendarmerie for dancing, drunkenly, around some fountain. It took our agent, Martin Hopewell, with all his powers of his limited schoolboy French to get Paul and Bruce released. John was not best pleased.

After watching The Damned I went with one of the tour crew, Nicky Tredwyn, to find a chemist. I bought some black hairdye and headed back to the hotel and got in the shower, two hours later emerging with a head of hair that looked like some stiff yard brush. Even though I scrubbed and scrubbed I couldn't wash off the black streaks that had run down and stained my face.

Back at the festival the atmosphere was brilliant. I got drunk and partied. I didn't get any sleep and in the morning I felt very ill. But I was still buoyed up by the whole event although I was not looking forward to the gig, and at the soundcheck I could hardly keep it together. Then there was some dispute over the billing order. The Jam had originally been billed to headline. As a result John told us to pack up and said that we were going home. I must admit, I did give a sigh of relief.

Around this time I was still living with my parents and when I walked in on that Sunday afternoon my dad was just taking a tray of tea and biscuits upstairs to my mum. My dad looked at me, said hello and continued in his task. As he climbed the stairs I heard him shout out: 'Paul's home and he has only gone and dyed his hair.' It must have ignited my mum's imagination because after a loud shriek she shot down the stairs to see for herself what horrors I had inflicted on myself. She sighed, thankful that my hair was just black and not green or orange.

A few days later, over a cup of tea, my mum said to me, 'Is the band not doing very well at the moment, it's just that you haven't been doing any other work recently either?' I was astounded, even after having been on the road mostly every day since the beginning of the year and having records out, playing in The Jam and living the life of a working musician and having a career in music was still very alien to both her and my dad. I think she was only reassured that some kind of career was possible when The Jam performed on *Top Of The Pops* for a second time, on August 18, for 'All Around The World'.

Outside of what was happening for The Jam there was also a lot of excitement going on around the Queen's Silver Jubilee. In many ways this period simply passed me by because I was too wrapped up with what was going in with the band. I wasn't especially for the Royals but by the same taken I wasn't against them either.

There was also all this stuff going on with reduced working weeks and strikes. Most of the disruption seemed to be happening in the big industries, like coal mining and power companies. It didn't seem to affect the south of England as much as it did the north. I suppose it reminded me of the three-day-week of a couple of years earlier. Britain in the mid-seventies had lived through the heatwave of 1976, harsh winters, blackouts and power cuts and there were periods when rubbish bags were stacked up on the streets because the dustmen were on strike. Yes, people in the late seventies were still carrying tensions.

Leading up to this period I was able to walk out of one job and pretty much walk into another, but this was changing. Fortunately, for me, having plenty of jobs available suited my lifestyle. I mean in the years building up to us getting signed to Polydor I was always on the edge of nearly losing my jobs. It was inevitable really because I was constantly diving off early on Friday afternoons and then arriving late on Monday mornings. And then once The Jam got signed I still didn't have the pressures of a family to look after or a mortgage and bills to keep on top of; I think the strikes impacted on the people that had those things to manage the most. There was an air of uncertainty about the future.

I was simply enjoying being young and being in a band. I just didn't have the same kind of responsibilities that I saw many others having to deal with. What I remember thinking about the Queen's Jubilee was how odd it was that a lot of money and investment was being poured into that but at the same time there was a great deal of strife going on between the government and the miners. There was a lot of social tension and in many ways this helped to launch the activist side of punk.

On the day 'In The City' was released we played a show at the Royal College of Art in London. Then going into May we had a load of shows lined up in towns and cities across the UK, among them Manchester and Edinburgh, and we also found ourselves having to deal with a series of cancellations at places like Wolverhampton, Stafford and Canterbury. June picked up again and we played something like 24 shows in that month alone. There would have been more but a couple were cancelled, including another at Chelsea Football Club's ground Stamford Bridge that for some reason never happened.

Now that Polydor wanted an album our contract with them was re-negotiated. We also had to visit the Polydor pressing factory. There had been some issue to do with the album insert and some of the factory workers refused to work with them; something to do with the swear words that they didn't like. In an attempt to show the workers that we were not a bunch of animals it was arranged that we would visit the factory and spend the day with them. Polydor thought it would be in our favour to show the workers, who had seen the Bill Grundy show, that we were not like the Pistols – all spitty and sweary. It didn't work and in the end the albums were released without the inserts. Those inserts are quite sought after these days; I have one at home somewhere.

However, what we did get out of the day was a bunch of records we grabbed from the shelves in the warehouse. But unlike the stories of The Clash filling their bags with free vinyl and selling them in the record shop around the corner, we kept ours. I gathered up loads, to the point where I couldn't physically carry any more.

I got some nice T. Rex albums that day; a refreshing relief from what was still being played on the radio and *TOTP*. I remember Paul, Bruce and me would often be moaning about what was getting played. The music from the sixties wasn't getting a look in, The Beatles were long gone and direction was lost. *TOTP* was sickly really. I think it turned us into grumpy old men before our time.

Around the time that 'In The City' came out bands were just starting to make videos and Polydor felt The Jam should make one. Obviously, 'In The City' was a certainty; then 'Art School' was selected. And, of course, it was all going to be done on a low budget.

We were taken to Pinewood film studios. While there we noticed the white Lotus Esprit from the James Bond film *The Spy Who Loved Me*. And we saw the set with the Fortress of Solitude from the *Superman* film. It was massive and made from polystyrene. I think the film had recently been finished because they were happy to allow people, myself included, to climb all over it.

The Jam were set up on a stage that would normally be used for shooting scenes for films. 'Art School' was an odd video really. The Carver brothers from Woking, Steve and Pete, even make an appearance, as did Paul's sister Nicky; they were filmed painting a blank sheet in pink and yellow paint. We had known the Carvers since school and they had supported us all the time, drinking with us in pubs like the Princess in Maybury. Pete went on to work the lighting at some Jam shows and Steve worked the merchandise stall and sold T-shirts. For that shoot, and it was unusual for us during this period, we are not wearing our black and white suits but were dressed more casually. I'm wearing a pink button-down shirt and Paul a black jumper with tape stuck to it. Both Paul and Bruce are also wearing white Sta-Prest trousers.

Then came our debut appearance on *Top Of The Pops*. For this we stuck to what we knew and wore our black and white outfits; I also wore sunglasses. Paul and Bruce swung their red and white Rickenbackers around whilst a couple of kids in the audience attempted to pogo. The rest of the audience, who were mainly entrenched in their seventies get-ups of big collar shirts, flares and longish hair, stood around like they were waiting in a bus queue. That was our *TOTP* debut.

'In The City' reached number 40 in the charts and this pleased Polydor and boosted their enthusiasm to get an album out. Songs like 'Art School', 'I've Changed My Address' and 'I Got By In Time' were good examples of the way The Jam worked in rehearsals. More often than not Paul would bring in an idea and we would get to work on it. Songs weren't rushed but we had a great work ethic and would just get on with creating and learning the song.

The majority of songs on the album were also Paul's first songwriting attempts that didn't include any input from Steve Brookes. They didn't need any either, because Paul had now found his direction and he was coming up with his own ideas.

'Slow Down' had been in the set for a long time and many of the songs on the album were played in that style because that was what we knew and had been playing for years. My drumming was pretty straightforward; it wasn't until 'The Modern World' that I started thinking about a more creative drumming approach, although I don't think this started to show until *All Mod Cons*.

In some ways I think this evolution applied to all three members of The Jam. Even at the time some critics said they thought we had been signed too early and we would have been a better band if we had been signed around the time of *All Mod Cons*. But then I think it was one of the strengths of The Jam; we never liked to stay still for too long. Plus, being just a three-piece I think we felt some restrictions and this in turn pushed us to want to explore new areas and stretch the musical boundaries. Also, one of the things we learnt, and we learnt this quite early on, was that being in a three-piece meant that there was nowhere to hide. If one of us stopped playing it was very noticeable. We tried to turn this into a virtue so that when one stopped it was done to maximum effect.

'Away From The Numbers' did have something to do with The Who – *The Who By Numbers*, their album, and their early name The High Numbers. The song had loads of Who influences in it. I think that song showed us scratching away at that particular heritage. It was all linked to the sixties mod thing. This was the track we struggled with most to record, taking a few takes to get right. I'm not sure we had even played it live before we recorded it; we didn't play it much live after either. I mean by the time *In The City* was up and running we had started working on *Modern World* and so there were always newer songs that found their way into the set.

'The Batman Theme' was also fun to do. The Who did a version of this – it was originally composed by Neal Hefti – on their *Ready Steady Who* EP in 1966 and I think we drew inspiration from that one day in a rehearsal. We just mucked around with it, sped it up and decided that we could do something with it and we could include it on the album. We liked the way the tune had that surf vibe and 12-bar blues progression. It also seemed to tie in with the pop art thing, the clothes and all the other visuals.

I think 'Sounds From The Street' caught the feel of all what was going on around us. It was us trying to give credibility to what was happening in the punk scene. It would have made a good single, but then I think a lot of Jam songs could have done.

'Non-Stop Dancing' was Paul's obvious nod to the soul records that he liked from the sixties. In the earlier Jam sets we'd included many American sixties soul tracks. 'In The Midnight Hour', of course, appeared on *Modern World*. We cut our teeth doing covers in The Jam. And even at the time of punk and what was going on in 1977 we weren't ashamed to cite our influences. The Jam was an honest band in that respect. If anything we made a point of standing up and telling people what our rock'n'roll influences were. We were proud that we liked The Kinks, The Who and the Wilson Picketts of the world. This went against the punk grain because many punk bands were anti everything that had gone before.

I think 'Time For Truth' is an early demonstration of Paul's 'angry young man' stance. Paul's lyrics were personal to him and only he truly knew their meanings. We always had Jam fans coming up to us and telling us how much they loved a particular lyric because of this reason and that reason. They would try to describe to me what a lyric meant to them, and on occasion I would tell Paul and Paul's response would be to tell them that he didn't have that in his mind at the time of writing it. But Paul wasn't knocking them, he was pleased that they could take his lyrics and relate them to their own situation in some way. This was certainly one of the strengths in Paul's songwriting; he could write something from his point of view, but it related to so much, to what so many other people, from that generation were feeling and experiencing.

There were certainly times when I would be influenced by some of Paul's lyrics and this would affect my drumming. An example would be the drum roll in 'Town Called Malice' or 'Down In The Tube Station At Midnight' when the part where the drums come back in sounds like a train 'echoing' down the track. Where possible I tried to make my drums link with the visuals of a lyric.

Finishing off the album was 'Bricks And Mortar', which funnily enough we did because of John's history within the building trade. I think Paul cleverly included some metaphors relating to 'this is how you build a house, this is how you build society and this is how you build your life'.

Pete Wilson, along with Chris Parry, helped us pull off a great album. By the time we were recording *All Mod Cons* we had a new producer in Vic Smith, but we did return to Pete for *The Gift* album in 1982. I think everyone that who worked with us in the studio did the band a great service, and as individuals I think we all drew a great deal of valuable experience from them. And each album was very different. *In The City* was simply a matter of capturing the band's live sound, the albums that followed were more studio orientated. After *In The City* we experimented more, and spent more time trying new things and tidying things up. I think we recorded all of *In The City* in 11 days, which was pretty quick really.

We tried to approach the recording of *Modern World* in the same way as *In The City* but it was a different ball game all together. I know that *Modern World* gets mixed reviews but I actually like the album. When it was first released some of the reviews were unfavourable, it wasn't what people had expected. It does have a different feel to *In The City*, but then this album was pretty much recorded in the studio and some of the songs weren't included in the live set for long if at all, whereas many of the songs on *In The City* had had time to be played live and in some cases for more than five years. Looking back, I think that whether or not it was a conscious thing, we moved on from *Modern World* quite quickly, possibly because of the press and the reaction from the record company over what they called 'disappointing sale figures'.

In between recording both of these albums we still gigged. And we started to notice familiar faces turning up at our soundchecks. From that period onwards fans would pick up on the band's routine of the day and they would arrive early in the afternoon to catch us soundchecking. We played all over London and Polydor made up loads of little badges with the venues written on them – The Jam at the Red Cow, The Jam at the Nashville and so forth – and we used to give these badges out. We were happy to have fans at those soundchecks and would certainly never have kicked anyone out. I don't think this was common practice among other bands at the time. Word must have spread because once we started to do shows outside of London fans in other towns and cities would show up at soundchecks too. There was always a few that tried to pull the trick of turning up for a soundcheck then nipping off to the toilets and hiding there until the doors opened in the evening. This never bothered us, and some of the lengths fans would go to and the places found to hide were very ingenious.

We got to know many of these fans well, we wouldn't necessarily know all their names, but we would say things like, 'I think I saw you at the 100 Club' or 'Didn't we have a chat at the Nashville?' It was impossible to remember everyone's names but faces we tended to remember.

During the day, when we were travelling or waiting for soundcheck time there was a hell of a lot of hanging around; our whole day now focused more than ever on the hour or so at the end of the day, the gig. On one occasion prior to a show at the Marquee, John, Paul and I were sitting in a pub in Wardour Street, killing time, while we waited for our equipment to be unloaded and set up, ready for our soundcheck. Without any warning a fight broke out, erupting like a small explosion in the pub. There were tables and chairs being thrown about everywhere. We nearly got caught up in someone else's brawl. John quickly pushed me and Paul out of the door just as things were starting to get really ugly. It was a stark reminder to us that London can be a hostile and volatile place.

On another afternoon a loud middle-aged American tourist wandered into one of our soundchecks at the Red Cow, looking for an afternoon drink. It was that short period in the afternoons when pubs had to close due to the licensing laws, and so, because the pub wasn't open for business, the barman couldn't sell him any beer. This, and the fact that we weren't playing any country & western songs in our soundcheck, annoyed the man. He started to hurl insults at us, complaining and griping about our songs and our playing ability. Our soundchecking fans retaliated and he had to make a hasty retreat from the pub. Jam fans were tough individuals, even back then, so I think that American tourist had a lucky escape.

Trouble wasn't an everyday event but sometimes it came our way. There was another incident when we all returned to our hotel after a show as we normally did, looking forward to a short spell relaxing with our girlfriends, to find the bar was full of Australian rugby players and their entourage, more than a little tipsy but in good spirits. Unfortunately they had transferred the serving of drinks for residents only to a small hatch in the lobby and a long queue was already forming. Several of us, including Paul, impatiently stood in line. I was sitting on a sofa at the other end of the lobby when we heard what sounded like a tray of drinks hitting the floor. Somebody had apparently turned around and knocked over Paul's drinks and an altercation had taken place resulting in what turned out to be one of the management for the rugby team receiving a cut to his head with a glass. The word soon got to the bar in the 'Chinese whisper' fashion that some 'punk rockers' had started a fight, so several of these large and well-oiled rugby blokes came blundering out to sort the situation. Before the police arrived, Bruce had received a beating and we had all sought refuge in our rooms. The police could not guarantee our safety and advised us to move to a different hotel. We were bundled out into the night to find alternative lodgings, small and very uncomfortable, as we had to take what we could find so late. Nobody got a good night's sleep or a drink.

Now The Jam had an album out and the need to promote it led to our first extended tour being organised and new people being employed. At first the entourage was quite small, then crew members Alan Belcher and Nicky Tredwyn were added and then

Dickie Bell was recruited as tour manager and to help John. Dickie came with a vast amount of touring experience, having worked with the likes of Judas Priest and later Iron Maiden. Countless shows were added and months went by in a blur of travelling, gigging and drinking.

There were shows that were organised with The Clash. The idea was that both bands would share equal billing. Bernie Rhodes was The Clash's manager and he didn't like the idea that we would share their PA. It wasn't even much of a PA system either, quite cheap, small and battered. And it wasn't really up to the size of the venues that we were booked into playing. So between the issues of the billing order and the PA and who was going to be paid the more money, things got out of hand and we pulled out of doing the shows. We were new to this sort of thing and didn't really have much understanding as regards what was happening. I was especially disappointed, and so when Polydor turned to us and told us that we didn't need to do the shows with The Clash and suggested we simply do our own tour instead, the disappointment turned into renewed confidence.

One show nestled in amongst all this touring was a support slot with The Stranglers at Leeds Polytechnic. I liked The Stranglers but saw them as being more of a pub rock band than a punk band. What they were doing was re-inventing themselves, just like us and The 101ers/Clash had done, into the new wave punk scene. They were much older than us and I think in that respect there was a degree of reverence for them from us.

Most of those at that Stranglers show, and many from that era, hadn't seen or heard of us. We played hard, fast and loud to that Leeds crowd, tearing through our set in the usual breakneck fashion. After our high-energy set The Stranglers still hadn't arrived. The crowd grew restless having been kept waiting for what seemed like ages. Eventually The Stranglers arrived and wandered on stage. They hadn't even had the luxury of soundchecking and it took them three or four numbers before their sound improved. The crowd was at risk of erupting but in the end things did settle down and I stood out front and watched them. And The Stranglers did sound great. They were one of the last bands that I was able to see in this way in the UK, that is being able to mix in with the crowd. It became too difficult afterwards. The last time I was able to wander out front was at a show we played at the Bracknell Sports Centre. It was also more a case of trying to be professional. I mean there were times when John would have to search the building and hunt us down, just to let us know that we would be going on stage in five minutes. In our early tours of the States it was totally different, we could walk around freely because nobody knew us.

Rehearsal time became more formal and began to focus on new material for the purpose of recording. We were also on the move all the time. In some ways soundchecks served as our rehearsal time when we were on the road. Some of the ideas for the *Modern World* album came out of soundchecks; then the rest was written in the studio. We didn't rehearse properly as a band until we moved into Nomis studios in Shepherd's Bush a year later.

I think there are some outstanding tracks on the *Modern World* album. I especially like 'Life From A Window'. I thought that was fabulous and worked well live when we revisited it years later playing with Bruce again in our band The Gift. And again this was an example of writing a song in the studio that only got better once it had been played in on the road. That was a song I wish we had spent time playing live first and then recorded. But, we just weren't able to do that. As far as the record company were concerned we needed to go on the road to promote the albums. We found ourselves always playing catch-up. Doing two albums in one year was a lot of work, plus we toured the UK and we ventured to the States for a whirlwind tour.

Some people didn't think that the *Modern World* album was very well thought out, and maybe that was true. We were just responding to what our new contract with Polydor was dictating. The *Modern World* album was also Bruce's first songwriting appearance. Both 'London Traffic' and 'Don't Tell Them You're Sane' were from Bruce. They found their way onto the album because we were short of material. I'm not saying they were bad songs, they are two good songs for the album, but because of time issues we needed enough songs to fill the album.

That's also why we included 'In The Midnight Hour'; drawing on what we had already in the live set. This would be repeated over the history of The Jam. When Polydor wanted a new single and we found ourselves short of new material we recorded 'David Watts'. It was still a great song to do and we were really pleased with it; it even motivated The Kinks to record a new version of it. We didn't see there was anything wrong in doing it. Remember Paul was under a lot of pressure to write songs to order and he didn't like that; but we had contractual obligations to meet. Record companies can be very pushy. They were always telling us that they need this or we need to do something because a deadline is coming up. So songs like 'In The Midnight Hour' or 'David Watts' served a purpose at the time. We had spent years playing covers, we enjoyed it and we were very good at it.

What we did learn, only after recording *Modern World,* was that we shouldn't have tried to record it in the same way as *In The City.* In those days Paul was quite impatient and would want the backing tracks laid down fairly quickly. This sometimes meant that when any guitar changes were made afterwards they didn't always line up with the bass and drums. Bruce and I learnt from this and by the time of recording *All Mod Cons* we would often routine long into the night, so that we at least were prepared and rehearsed as much as we could before recording the backing tracks the following day. Paul had his own routine and preferred to be out of the studio by six because he liked to get home to watch *Coronation Street.*

It was only after we had two albums out that we were in a position to start giving ourselves some sort of a wage. It wasn't much mind, just a few quid each month that paid for fags and beer. We didn't need much because we were either on the road or in the studio. Also the budget for such things as hotels was limited. The way it worked was that John and Dickie shared a room, I shared with Bruce and Paul shared with Gill Price, his girlfriend at the time. More often than not the hotels were shabby affairs with shared bathrooms and toilets located way down the corridor. However there was one hotel in Sheffield where we stayed that actually provided a shower unit. This was a rare treat that we were going to take advantage of. The only thing was that we had to fix it together to actually make use of it. Bruce lost his patience and had a battle with it. I can't remember who won but after this the road crew awarded him the nickname 'Shower Unit', but this only lasted until it was replaced with 'Shirley'.

The crew gave us all nicknames. Paul was known as 'Saddle Bags' because his cardigan pockets were always filled with items like cigarettes, lighters and cards. The crew called me 'Blind Boy' because I wore shades on stage but this was better than 'Pube' which I mysteriously inherited from Steve Brookes. Wearing shades wasn't always the brightest idea... ha ha! There was one gig at the Nashville were I had mislaid my bins and was handed an untried substitute pair. The problem was that they were so dark I could hardly find my way around the drum kit. I even had to grope my way across the stage to find the kit. Shortly after that experience I stopped wearing shades on stage.

Modern World was released in November and some of the immediate press reviews were disappointing. The initial sales weren't that great either. The band left the UK to play a couple of shows; one in Sweden and the other in Amsterdam at the Paradiso Club. In Amsterdam the audience were great and I remember it fondly as one of my all-time favourite shows.

Following those European shows a short, exploratory, but intensive visit to America was organised and we played at the famous Whisky A Go Go in Los Angeles on October 8. It was planned that we would play two shows a night at each of four venues. That meant in total we played eight shows during a 10-day visit. The record label had also organised press calls and photo shoots and they had us standing on tops of buildings with swimming pools in Los Angeles and all sorts of things. There were also interviews with the press in every town we went to. They were very keen to meet us, because by this time the whole British punk thing had filtered into the States. American journalists always kept a close eye on what was going on in the UK. Another thing about this whistle-stop tour of the States was that we only had one suit each. This meant that because we wore them on every show, they never properly dried out. The suits were dreadful, sweaty, smelly and damp and we had to walk about talking to people in those suits. The reps we met from the record company were all up and buzzy, but we were anything but.

Next we played at the Old Waldorf Club in San Francisco, but we had problems. During the soundcheck Paul kept getting electrical shots off the microphone. Try as they could the stagehands couldn't resolve the problem enough to satisfy Paul so John 'pulled the show'. The management pleaded with John, informing us that 'lots of other bands had survived the shows' but it was too late and we left and made our way to Boston and played at the Rathskeller, and then onto New York where we were booked to play at the famed CBGB.

The full name for the club was Country, Bluegrass and Blues, but there was also the OMFUG part which stood for Other Music for Uplifting Gormandizers. Local man Hilly Kristal had occupied 315 Bowery in one of the roughest and seediest parts of Manhattan since 1969 but it wasn't until 1973 that he changed the club's name to CBGB. During the club's lifetime it certainly left its mark on the history of rock'n'roll. Sadly, the club closed in 2006 and Kristal died the following year. Nowadays there is a restaurant on the premises.

What I remember most about CBGB is the cramped dressing room and being visited by one of The Ramones. I don't know which one it was as they all looked the same, same hair, same jeans and biker jackets. He came into the dressing room and sat himself down on the electric heater and then a few minutes later leapt up because he had burnt his arse on it. Patti Smith also popped in to say 'hi'. I didn't meet Blondie, another CBGB legend, on this occasion, but I did meet Debbie Harry at a party back in London, held on one of the big houseboats in Chelsea. I think Blondie may even have been living on the boat at the time. Many music industry types and band members were there, Paul, Bruce and me, two of the Sex Pistols – Paul Cook and Steve Jones – and there was Debbie Harry, but she didn't mix with everyone, preferring to keep herself to herself.

I was disappointed with CBGB because it was quite small and not how I thought it would be. Everyone was raving about the club being the New York version of London's Marquee, but it was nothing like the Marquee. If anything the Marquee was a step up from this small New York club with its neon signs placed all along the bar, the only lighting in the place. The stage was small too but the venue was crowded. I remember reading graffiti and stickers on the walls around the club and there just seemed to be mess everywhere. The toilets were to be avoided too, if you could manage it.

Those New York or American punk bands were totally different to us British ones. The Ramones and Blondie were more 'poppy and polished' really and didn't have that anger that British bands had as a default setting. I'm not sure why as New York in 1977 was in financial difficulties and drugs and violence were everywhere. What was going on in the States was a musical revolution just like what was happening in the UK, with lots of new talent coming through. They were doing their bit to break the mould of these huge arena type acts, bands like the Stones and Led Zeppelin and singers like Elton John and Rod Stewart who had dominated the seventies. Those acts were living up with the gods and there was nothing in between, and punk bands were changing that. We decided to make it our own scene and there was a great outpouring of brilliant new talent. CBGB acted as a launch pad for many of them in the same way the Marquee did back in the UK. Punk was a term used in American prisons back in the twenties and thirties but its origins might also go back to India and the punkawallas, who were the lowest of the low, at the bottom of the class system, who would spend hours operating fans to keep the wealthy happy and cool. And so back in the late seventies punks in New York or

London were the dirt and those on the ground level. We didn't care.

We didn't get much time to spend being a tourist in any of those American cities where we played. I do have a vague memory of leaving the hotel in New York to go and get some food. I had to buy food outside the hotel because I couldn't afford to buy any inside. I found a deli and bought some sandwiches and bottles of beer and had to smuggle them inside my coat, back into the hotel. I also remember that me, Nicky Tredwyn and Alan Belcher sneaked out to a bowling alley. We had decided that while in New York we just had to experience a proper New York bowling alley. It seemed that we found the filthiest bowling alley in the city because when we returned we were covered in grease and dirt. I told myself this was not how I imagined America to be, it just wasn't like I had seen it portrayed on the television.

The Jam did return to New York in the years that followed and in 2008 I went back with From The Jam. On this occasion we managed to stay in New York for four days. This time I explored New York with a greater appreciation of the city and I did the tourist trail and checked out Grand Central Station, Central Park, the Statue of Liberty and, of course, I ended up in Macy's.

CHAPTER FIVE

After *This Is The Modern World* we started to notice the roles of those assigned by Polydor to look after the business side of the band's interests. There were accountants with whom we always had to discuss funding and this usually caused conflict, their sole interest being to balance the books and sell the products that The Jam was producing, which was, of course, their job. But it often felt like it was us, the artist, versus them, the corporates. This tension would especially wind up Paul. It was simple, we were the band, the artists, and the musicians with our aims and goals, and their agenda often differed from ours. We were only interested in playing music, recording, doing shows and putting records out and this was our job, and we now had to understand that this was no longer a weekend passion. It had become a much more serious business for us.

By this time The Jam had been in the music business, properly, for a good year. During this time we were learning how to deal with and handle the types of people that worked within the industry. This was happening naturally alongside our main concern, rehearsing, continuing to produce good songs and playing our gigs well. We understood that by doing this, and concentrating on this, we would be fulfilling the demands placed on us by the industry.

This was how we handled Polydor and their accountants. We learnt to put up with them battering us with their demands 'to sell more products'. That was their job, we were not the salesmen – *we* were the product.

I personally, and I think Paul and Bruce felt the same, never felt employed by Polydor, in the traditional sense; if anything, we felt that the record label was there to work alongside the band. Two sides of the same coin. But when it comes down to it, it is a two-way street; it's just that one side of the street doesn't always see the others side's point of view and this is when there were problems.

By the end of 1977 and going into 1978 Polydor Records was very much a part of our lives and we were contractually bound to each other. We were also sharing the label with other bands, such as Sham 69, who we would sometimes see in the offices. It was odd though really, because even though you shared a record label with them, you don't always feel like you're on the same team with them. In fact, in those early Polydor days we didn't really bump into many of the other bands or get a chance to get to know them, because they would be out on the road at the same time as us. Occasionally our paths might cross if we were on the same bill at a festival or something. The Reading Festival was one such occasion when both The Jam and Sham 69 were playing but what really sticks in my mind about that festival was seeing Steve Hillage of Gong getting up on stage with Sham and playing a song with them. That seemed strange to me because Steve Hillage, great guitarist as he was, was from an entirely different musical universe to Sham 69.

I once had an encounter with Jimmy Pursey in the Polydor A&R offices in Stratford Place, where our A&R man Dennis Munday and producer Chris Parry and a load of the secretaries worked. Dennis was a great bloke who took over the A&R responsibilities from Chris, and he became really involved with The Jam and did a lot for us. Any band that is signed needs a good A&R man to stand between them and the record company and Dennis served us well in that sense. He really was a great help and we trusted him. Dennis started to get involved just as we were entering the *All Mod Cons* period.

Sometimes I would just hang out at the Polydor offices. On one of those days I was there and Jimmy was also there, Sham 69 had just released a new record. He was playing their record over and over again, and as soon as it ended, he would pick up the needle and start it again and continue dancing around, obviously pleased with his latest creation. I could see that the office staff were trying to work and thinking 'For god's sake Pursey shut up.' But they couldn't really do or say anything. It wasn't the done thing to upset the artist! But it didn't matter because I'd had enough anyway, so I strolled over to the record player and purposefully rammed the stylus right across his record, removed it from the deck and flung it at him. Only after I did that did it cross my mind that he was a taller bloke than me – oops I thought. His reaction was to glare at me and storm out of the office. There was a moment of tension. I suspect the office staff were grateful.

I did like Sham 69 but I know Paul Weller regarded them as a bit of a joke band. Once they started to run out of their early material, which was good, they got into their 'Hurry Up Harry' phase. I just don't think that stuff was particularly musically engaging. It was more novelty records. Out of all the Sham members it was Dave Parsons who I got to know the best, more so in the Time UK days via Jimmy Edwards, who was Sham's musical director and worked closely with Dave. Jimmy Edwards also released an acoustic version of 'In The City', and acted as a songwriter for Polydor, but it was through this connection that my friendship with Dave Parsons really came about.

Going into the *All Mod Cons* period the accountants were smiling because the jam pot of money was filling up. Money was often the area of friction, mostly because the albums sometimes ran over budget and that rang alarm bells at Polydor. At the end of the first meeting with our accountants, we were given a pep talk on how important it was to be open and clear about our financial arrangements with each other. Pointing out that it may not seem relevant now, when we were starting out, but that it might do in the future should there be a dispute. Of course we never believed that we would fall into such a trap at the time.

But there was money around and there were ideas of how it could be spent. One example came from one of the art directors. It was suggested that it might be a good idea to emboss the laurel surround on *Setting Sons*. Polydor went along with the idea but then decided it wasn't such a great idea because it cost too much so they put a limit of 100,000 copies and all those album sleeves printed after that were flat. For us, as the band, we just wanted it embossed, we liked the idea, we didn't really care if it cost more money to press them up, and that sort of stuff simply wasn't our concern, although if I remember correctly the extra cost was set against our royalty.

As well as these areas of friction, there would be other cock-ups. An example of this was when the label pressed up copies of *Setting Sons* but somehow managed to print a batch of covers that didn't include the track listing. So instead of binning them and starting again, they printed up stickers of the track list and someone had to stick them on the back instead.

Alongside the frictions and not always seeing eye-to-eye with Polydor on occasion, during 1978 there was the ever increasing added pressure of having to come up with new material. This was partly how 'News Of The World', one of Bruce's songs, came about. The situation was that Bruce could, and wanted to, write some songs for The Jam. So during one of those periods of pressure we decided to opt for one of Bruce's songs, and this turned out to be 'News Of The World'. Following this release we agreed on a cover song, which turned out to be 'David Watts'; in effect this was simply to meet Polydor's demands and deflect some of the pressure.

The only problem with Bruce writing songs was that they were instantly – and I think unfairly – compared by the press to Paul's songs and I think this was something Bruce never really recovered from. Bruce wasn't Paul and Paul wasn't Bruce, but both were members of The Jam. We understood why the press and some people thought the way they did. What this did mean was that the songwriting from here on really fell onto Paul's shoulders alone and that's where it remained until the last days of the group. It was simply something that Paul had to live with. He hated being treated like a machine that was expected to keep churning out songs to order, and recording songs like 'David Watts' helped sometimes.

Also, Paul wasn't the sort of songwriter who would write something that he hadn't put his heart and soul into. I think Paul had made the decision that he was only going to put out great songs and he saw the value in that and wasn't going to make any compromises in this area. Thankfully he didn't. That was one of the great things about Jam songs. They were all of a great quality.

On August 26, 1978 we released 'David Watts', written of course by Ray Davies, backed with '"A" Bomb In Wardour Street', which reached number 25 in the charts. This entire period was an explosive time: the world was still in the shadow of the Cold War and the IRA was still a very active presence, jobs were scarce and there was a great deal of political tension the length and breadth of Great Britain.

'"A" Bomb In Wardour Street' had various meanings. Yes, there was still this threat of an atomic war hanging over everyone. I remember growing up and thinking, 'I'm going to be really pissed off if somebody drops the bomb and I haven't even got into my thirties.' There were a lot of people who felt a lot of angst. A couple of years later, on October 23 at the Rainbow in Finsbury Park and then on the 24th on the Embankment, we played CND benefit shows. Paul was especially aware of this 'A bomb' topic. The politics of it all also affected many people, and I'm sure that to some extent The Jam helped raise the awareness of this in many young people.

What 'David Watts'/'"A" Bomb In Wardour Street' did was demonstrate that The Jam was moving on. By the time the single came out we had been back to America, playing some disaster gigs with the Blue Öyster Cult, more shows at CBGB and we had a couple of shows in Canada too. Back in the UK the summer had been reasonably quiet on the gigging front, though we did play the

Reading Festival, but we didn't really do any intensive touring until November. In fact it was on November 29 that we were booked to play the Great British Music Festival at the Wembley Empire Pool. That was an unexpected billing to say the least because of who we shared the billing with – Generation X and Slade.

The Jam did a lot of gigging during the years that we were signed to Polydor. We played at venues of all shapes and sizes. In 1979 we decided to play two gigs under false names. The first was at the Marquee Club in London on November 2 when there was some trouble and the club's glass doors were smashed. We called ourselves John's Boys. The second was the following night at the Nashville, London and for this we went under the name The Eton Rifles. Both gigs were 'open secrets' and the word had got out and both were very well attended.

Our thinking behind doing these gigs was our way of revisiting those types of venues where we had learnt our trade really. After those two gigs we pretty much played solidly throughout the remainder of November and right through December. Many of the shows we played were to promote a single or an album so doing gigs as 'John's Boys' and 'Eton Rifles' was just us filling a gap. As a working band, either on the road or in the studio, we had to think up ways to fill gaps. And The Jam simply loved to play live, our date sheet between 1977 and 1982 pretty much full up. We weren't one of those bands that made an album, then toured to promote it, then took six months off. We constantly went from one thing to the next, studio or tour. We did one tour which we called the Bucket and Spade tour, visiting seaside towns and as John pointed out to me, our driver's surname was Bucket and another crew member, Joe Awome, was black. It wasn't a racist thing at all, just a reflection of the terminology of the time.

During 1978 we started to notice that our crowd was changing. For the first year we were seen as a punk band, then we were called new wave and then the second generation of mods started to arrive, lots of them, and we became known as a mod band. By the time *All Mod Cons* was released our old black suits with white shirts and black ties look was a distant memory. It's funny really to think how much can change in a matter of just a few months.

Sponsorship was partly responsible for the way we, as a band, started to look; more for Bruce and me anyway. Paul was always very aware of the mod thing and managed to align us with sponsors with whom we were comfortable. Some were based in shops down Carnaby Street and the surrounding areas. The main two were Melandi, who did the shirts and jumpers, and Shelly's, which sold Jam footwear, the bowling, stage and cycling shoes, in black and white, or red, white and blue, or black and blue. I don't think they started out as Jam shoes, it was simply a matter of me, Paul and Bruce liking the shoes; then after that, they became known as 'our shoes' or 'Jam shoes'.

I never thought those shoes were particularly mod in the true sense of what mod was, but they were part of the American bowling fashion back in the sixties. In the late seventies this was the look that the kids adopted for their footwear. Grant Fleming, from the East End, had a lot to do with helping to kick-start that seventies mod revival. The new mods still kept the jackets and the parkas, though, and of course the button-down shirts. This was a very sixties mod thing and Melandi did a good range of shirts. The shop was run by two guys, Mel and Andy, which is how the shop's name came about. Shops like this really helped to strengthen both The Jam's image and our fans' image. These fans felt an affinity with towns like Brighton and Margate and those who were old enough rode Vespas and Lambrettas, seeking out seaside resorts that related to mod history. Then, of course, they needed their rivals and in the late seventies these were either skinheads or punks. It was a very serious affair and our fans had to keep their wits about them at all times. There were numerous occasions where mods got chased around the streets of Soho, or the mods chased someone else. It was around this time that the film of The Who's *Quadrophenia* was released too, and that chimed in with the whole mod revival thing.

We also wore Union Jack jackets, but we weren't the first to do this. The Who wore them first back in the mid-sixties, and playing the *Batman* theme was also something The Who had done. For The Jam it all related to that sixties thing; that pop art thing. Using picture sleeves for our singles hadn't been done since the sixties, as this was dropped in the seventies in favour of advertising the record label's name instead.

Carnaby Street really did get its second wind in the late seventies. I remember the day the photo on the back cover of 'News Of The World' was taken. Paul looks very moody. A big fan of the Steve Marriott look, he understood the importance of detail, how a 'serious' mod would need to look to carry off the image properly. Paul even tried seersucker shirts but I think he found them too effeminate; a bit too Austin Powers for Paul. Bruce preferred to dress in clothes similar to Paul but I decided not to just copy, so I wore a black leather jacket. I've also got on a target jumper that was made for me by a fan. I think I also wore winkle-picker boots. I was going for more of that Rolling Stones look rather than The Small Faces. Certainly from the time we dropped the black suits we began to develop our own identities.

It's a shame that Carnaby Street had become such a tourist establishment. During its heyday, it boasted a marvellous collection of boutiques. The shop windows looked spectacular, the coloured paving stones had been added, some shops had been there for several years, some even had clubs in their basements, like the Roaring Twenties Club below number 50 Carnaby Street that played a lot of ska music in the sixties. Don Arden had offices above one of the shops in the street during the time he managed The Small Faces. There's a great deal of history that relates to British music and British fashion in Carnaby Street. Sadly, these days, it has lost most of its charm and the excitement it once had.

So these same mods that started to turn up at Jam gigs would also flock to the mod mecca that was Carnaby Street to buy their shirts, shoes and parkas. Parkas were a big thing. One of my most vivid memories was seeing a load of mods clad in their parkas at the soundcheck at one of our shows in France; the Pavillon Baltard in Paris in 1981. By this time parka-wearing mods were in full force and they were organising coaches to follow us across Europe. At the venue there was a huge row of benches at the back filled with mods all wrapped up in their green parkas. Kenny Wheeler, another of our roadies, would refer to them as the Muppets because they reminded him of the puppet audience from *Sesame Street*. That was only Kenny having a bit of fun. We thought it was great that our fans followed us across Europe and had their own identity. The Jam was becoming as important to them as it was to us, and this just grew.

By late 1978 some things started to separate out, with fans of The Clash distancing themselves from fans of The Jam. Several of the bands that had come out of last year's punk movement were moving on and making their own mark, they and their fans going their own way. This country can be so tribal with its music and fashion and this meant that punks only listened to punk bands, skinheads only listened to skinhead bands and the mods... well, they listened to The Jam of course. If you were into heavy metal you wore a leather jacket, skinheads wore flight jackets and mods wore their parkas. These tribes had very defining boundaries.

By 1978 other bands were coming through that dressed like us and shared the same influences, and these included The Chords, Secret Affair, The Lambrettas and The Jolt. It was interesting for me to see those bands appear but we didn't feel part of this mod revival thing. In some ways, we felt it was quite flattering and we always liked to see bands starting up and having a go. The punks had opened up the field, allowing all kids to start up bands and there was a great deal of excitement around during that period. Also, pubs were prepared to present live music again, rather than relying on discos that played recorded music. So it was OK to see bands springing up and following in our footsteps, just as it was seeing bands forming and taking their lead from the Pistols or The Clash. It was a healthy time for live music in the UK.

One band that was unfairly compared with The Jam was The Jolt, a Scottish band that was signed to Polydor for a while. Although influenced by the new wave, punk or whatever you want to call it, they had their own sound. But that whole period didn't seem to last for long and some of those bands came and went pretty quickly. Because we were a busy working band we simply didn't see a lot of what was going on with other bands. We read about it, but our paths rarely crossed. So, I can't really say if The Jolt were any good or not. What I did know is that the people that went to see The Jam also went to see The Chords and Merton Parkas and bands like this.

Credit to some of those bands however, such as Generation X because they evolved, moved to the States and Billy Idol did very well with his career. Many artists and bands did survive the punk years and the mod thing, people like Elvis Costello, The Stranglers and Madness are still knocking around.

Once The Jam really took off Bruce, Paul and myself were no longer fans of other bands any more; the mystery was gone, we were the band, and we were the ones caught up in it. We just didn't get the time, like we used to, to be fans of other bands. Some things don't change however, and even today when I go to a gig, I watch the drummer, and I'll keep an eye on the road crew to see if they're making any mistakes. I never really wanted to lose that sense of mystery that surrounds bands. I enjoyed the mystery of wondering what they got up to back stage and on their days off. I think many fans fantasise about it, and most will get it totally wrong anyway. But by being in The Jam and in the music industry, much of that mystery was unwrapped and the charm was broken.

Following the release of 'News Of The World' there was more pressure from the record label to come up with more songs and Polydor booked us into the Farmyard Rehearsal Studios, which was stuck out in Suffolk, in the middle of nowhere. The idea was that by being in this remote place we would concentrate on writing songs with no distractions like drinking, which was a big deal for us. We were always going to the pub after rehearsals or recording and Polydor's thinking was that by sticking us in that isolated studio we would have nothing to do but knuckle down.

When we arrived the digs and the rehearsal studio were still being built. It was owned by Trevor Morais, the drummer with a jazzy pop group called The Peddlers who had a few minor hits in the sixties after escaping from the Merseybeat scene in Liverpool. There we were, dumped in this half-finished place, thinking what the fuck! We set up our gear in one of the Portakabins with all the best intentions, and then we set about finding out where the nearest pub was. This turned out to be way too far away, too far to walk and we had no car, and we also discovered that the only food they could muster up would be a sandwich. The accommodation at the farm was basic and we had to make our way across the building site to the main house in the morning to get showered. We stuck it out for two days and eventually we marched over to a phone box and phoned John Weller. 'Help! Come and get us,' was the message.

We just didn't need this sort of arrangement. During those couple of days, we did, at best, rehearse for only a couple of hours each day. That's how we were, that's how we worked. When we played together things would come together quite easily. As a musical unit Paul, Bruce and I were quite efficient. But once we had produced a song, learnt it, shaped it, dropped bits in and out of it, it was done. There was no point just keep going over and over it.

We returned to London and went into Polydor's own studios to demo up our new material. Using Polydor's facilities was a quick means to an end. It was cheap, they had their own in-house engineer and it served to get demos recorded. Over the years we did many of these sessions.

Countless bootlegs of Jam recordings have surfaced since The Jam split up, some more readily available than others, and some with far better quality sound than others. I once came across a collection of these demos that included several songs that I couldn't even remember doing. Some songs showed up on a bootleg compilation called *The Jam Extras* and that's OK. That comp includes some covers like 'Get Yourself Together' and 'Move On Up', but on the set of demos I heard there were versions of us playing 'Waterloo Sunset',

'Stand By Me' and a Brenton Wood track called 'I Think You've Got Your Fools Mixed Up'. I don't even think this was The Jam at all. Indeed, it sounded more like some early recordings of The Style Council. There was a female voice in the recording too which made me think it was perhaps DC Lee. But I certainly didn't recognise it as being anything to do with The Jam.

The version of 'Stand By Me' had a keyboard part on it that I suspect was being played by Paul. He may even have been playing the drums, which he would do sometimes. He liked to mess around on the drum kit and in the end I even bought him a set of his own. This happened when we were on a tour of the States, during which Paul celebrated a birthday. I thought it would be a good idea to get him a drum kit as a present so I contacted Premier Drums and arranged for a small kit to be delivered, not to our hotel but for it to be left waiting for him back in England. I actually had the drums delivered to Nomis Studios before we left for the States and had a cheesy photograph taken of me stood behind the kit pointing at it. I placed the photo in with Paul's birthday card. On the day of his birthday we had a bit of a party in the hotel. I found a moment to give Paul the card which he took, opened, thanked me for and then just sort of threw to one side. This left me feeling quite miffed at the time, but he obviously hadn't realised the significance of the photo and what my present to him really was. He may have been just a bit pissed and it hadn't registered.

The party went on and on but I slipped away and went to bed. I'd only been in my room for a few minutes when there was a knock on the door. It was Paul. It turned out that John had scolded him about not showing more appreciation for my present and sent him up to my room to thank me. Paul explained that he just hadn't realised and everything was fine.

The version on the demos of 'Waterloo Sunset' also didn't sound like me playing the drums. It could have been Paul playing everything, including the bass on it. Remember he did start out as The Jam's bass player.

Some of the demos being pushed around credit the songs with certain titles that I don't recognise at all, and I don't know where they come from. One title was 'Not Far At All'; maybe this was a working title for a short period but the tune sounded like 'Tales From The Riverbank', so it's possible that's what that evolved into. The demo sounds like it's a work in progress and we are trying to figure out what worked and what didn't. We would have a tune and ask ourselves if this part was too fast, or too slow, or whether it should be shifted to a different place in the song.

There was an instrumental on the demos titled 'The Sweeney', with loads of experimental guitar noises, feedback and what have you on it, and a lot of an open hi-hat beat. I have no recollection of doing this tune but it did sound like it had remnants of another Jam song, so maybe the best part of that instrumental was lifted and used in a different song. The thing is we spent a lot of time in the studio jamming as well as playing songs. Sometimes they would get recorded, sometimes they wouldn't. Perhaps sometimes we didn't know if we were being recorded or not. We threw a lot of ideas around in the studio. Sometimes we would work on something but at some point all decide it was rubbish and simply discard it, or we would just keep the bit we liked. Then we might shelve it until it reappeared in another song somewhere along the line.

I think these demos gave rise to the myth of the supposed lost Jam album. There never was a lost album, but there were plenty of songs we worked on but never used or just simply became a part of a whole new song. Chris Parry would tell us when something wasn't working or gelling and we would listen to him. We could be very critical about we did as a band and work a song for ages until it was finished. Sometimes we would just lift a hook or a drum part and drop it in somewhere else. Often Paul would come in with just a lyric and say, 'I got this but I just don't know what to do with it' so we would work with it and sometimes something would emerge and a song would be created. 'Funeral Pyre' began as just the drums and bass, then Paul fitted in his guitar and lyrics over what we were doing.

But we did work quickly in the studio and we did record many sessions because it was good to lay them down so we could return to them at some point later on. The other important thing to remember is that because we were a three-piece we really had to work hard to fill up all the spaces in a song. As soon as one of us dropped out of a song it became pretty bloody obvious.

So that song title 'Sweeney' is one where I have no idea where it came from. It sounds to me like something we worked on but dropped and just used a part of the lick in a different song at some point. The guitar sounds on it make me think it came from the *Absolute Beginners* period of The Jam.

On the demo there was an early version of 'Shopping', only it's titled 'Catch A Flame' or 'This Flame'. I'm using brushes just as I did on 'Shopping', but I found using them difficult because I wasn't used to them. This song came about because Paul had come across some jazz record that included a flute which inspired him to want to try something similar with The Jam, and it was because he wanted to capture a jazz type feel that it was suggested I experiment with brushes rather than sticks. So I did. I was surprised I even owned any brushes; playing with them needs a completely different technique than playing with wooden sticks. The guy I had been to see Buddy Rich with as a kid was a very talented drummer and I picked up a few tips about drumming from him. He'd explained to me how old jazz drummers created a swirling and hissing snare drum sound just using brushes, and showed me how with their left hand they move the brush smoothly around the white battered drum skin in a circular fashion and by doing so build up that unique sound. The right hand then punctuates the hissing with the beats, which gives it that jazz feel. It's a bit like rubbing your stomach in circles going one direction and tapping the top of your head at the same time.

Another song was titled 'Simon', probably a good example of one of those mystery songs from the so-called lost album. This sounded like it could have been from the 1978/79 Jam period as it didn't have the brashness of the early days or the feel of the last two albums. It was over 30 years since I last heard this song and I have no idea why it wasn't a song we pursued. It does betray our influences, with The Who clearly in there. I know we were all very impressed with The Who's *Meaty Beaty Big And Bouncy* hits compilation and we drew inspiration from it. This album was The Who's great sixties singles, all short sharp songs, before they moved into rock opera and their seven or eight minute mega rock songs like 'Won't Get Fooled Again'. Lots of influences rubbed off on us over our years together and I remember Paul digging out something by The Action and playing it to us. I hadn't even really heard anything by The Action but Paul had sourced them and liked what they had done in their sixties mod days.

Other songs on that collection of demos were versions of James Brown's 'I Feel Good', 'I Got My Mojo Working', which is more of a jamming session with Dave Liddle, and 'Be Bop A Lula', the Gene Vincent song that Paul seemed to enjoy singing. There were also recordings that I suspect was not The Jam playing at all but members of the crew. Sometimes they would pick up our instruments and play for a bit of fun, especially after they'd got back from the pub, just like we did.

Another track was one that had been titled 'Worlds Apart'. There was loads of piano on it, which Paul would have played. This was a good example of a riff developing into another song and in this instance the hook line found its way into 'London Girl'. Instead of Paul singing 'La la la la la worlds apart' he ended up singing, 'La la la la la London girl'. A song titled 'Along The Grove' had similarities to 'Liza Radley', the B-side of 'Start'. It's all Paul strumming away on a crunching guitar and singing, so I think this was an early attempt at that song. There was also a track with Bruce on vocals titled 'Best Of Both Worlds'. This eventually appeared on the *All Mod Cons* deluxe edition but it could have resurfaced earlier as inspiration for 'News Of The World'. It certainly sounds from that period.

'Walking In Heaven's Sunshine' was another track that sounded very sixties influenced but when I heard it, it didn't ring any bells at all. Again, it may not have been a Jam track as I had by now come to realise that just because a song had found its way onto a Jam demo it doesn't mean it's actually a Jam recording. One of the songs on the demo had the title 'Long Hot Summer', which of course was a Style Council song that came out the year after The Jam had split up. On the demo it's mostly all wistful guitar and piano accompanied by Paul singing something about a long hot summer storm. But I don't recall this song so this was possibly an early Style Council song. Some songs from the time when The Jam were together did carry over to the Style Council, 'A Solid Bond In Your Heart' an obvious example.

Yet another song on the demo featured versions as an instrumental and with both male and female vocalists. Paul did the male vocals but the female may have been Tracie Young or one of the members of Bananarama who had at times supported us – they weren't a great hit with Jam fans – or Afrodiziak which was made up of Caron Wheeler and Claudia Fontaine, who did the backing vocals for The Jam on our last tour. The song was called 'Dr Love' and wasn't that far away from a new romantics type tune. It was of the time I suppose. The instrumental version employed the use of an 808 drum machine and a keyboard. Both Bananarama and Tracie went on to cover it.

There were so many riffs and beginnings of songs that we would throw down, but as quickly as we threw them down we would as quickly discard them. We were always looking forward and moving on. We were good at focussing on what was in front of us. And some of the stuff we recorded in the studio just wasn't meant for public consumption. Not everything is of a quality that should appear in the public domain.

After the reality check from Chris Parry, who told us we really needed to make a greater effort for the third album, studio time was booked and recording got under way during the summer of 1978, at Eden Studios in Chiswick and RAK Studios in St Johns Wood. Vic Smith had by this time taken the main role of producer from Chris Parry as well because a 'too many cooks' situation was developing. The RAK Studios weren't the biggest in the world but they had a great reputation as they had been owned by Mickie Most, who produced scores of big hits during the sixties. I remember this period as being very optimistic, despite our realisation that things were now getting serious. We knew that we needed to 'come up with the goods'. And what we heard a lot was, 'If you haven't cracked it by your third album, then you never will.' The pressure that Paul had been feeling earlier was now falling on all three of us, not only on stage, where we felt the most at home, but also in the studio and from the media too.

Chris Parry took us to one side and told us in no uncertain terms that we needed to work harder and we needed to come up with a great third album; a world class album that would sell. He challenged us and told us that we just can't just go through the motions; it had to be better, 'we' had to be better.

We set about recording the songs that had been demoed in previous sessions. But the rumours of a so called 'lost' third album are simply not true. We re-worked a lot of songs and it was working for us. During those recordings everybody pulled out all the stops; everyone really did work harder. Bruce and I spent a lot of time working out arrangements. I think Bruce and I realised there was a lot more that we could put into the songs and this was what was needed to do to make the third album different and better than the previous two. Paul, or any band's main songwriter, can put a song on the table, but without the band actually making it work and pulling it all together, a song's potential is greatly limited.

There was something different about the way we did the third album, about the creativity that went into it. As a band we discovered new ways to go about putting songs together. Also, Vic Smith's production skills were a great motivation to us. 'Tube Station' just wouldn't have been finished if it wasn't for his encouragement and helping us to explore new possibilities. Paul was having doubts about the song and was unsure that it should even be included. He got ever so frustrated because whatever we tried it just didn't seem to be working. Thankfully Vic thought the song was really good and pushed us on. Eventually we did get it recorded, doing it in three sections which Vic pulled together. I don't think we ever revisited this approach to recording, but it did work for 'Tube Station'. Yes, Vic did a great job stitching those three parts together in the studio; and it turned out to be one of The Jam's best loved songs.

Then there was the drum fill section that seemed to excite the crowd at gigs. Sometimes that fill went on longer than on the recording because Paul would walk off stage. There was a cue to let Bruce and Paul know when they needed to come back in, but sometimes they would ignore it and leave me to continue playing. I would often be sat there thinking, 'Where the fuck has Paul gone… he's gone off for a fag' or 'Where's Bruce? He's gone off to change his trousers again.' Bruce was always tearing the arse out of his trousers so he would dive off the stage at the first opportunity and grab the spare pair that he kept at the side of the stage. I don't think the audience ever really saw this because his front faced them but his backside faced me. On many occasions Bruce started the gig with one pair of trousers but finished with a different pair.

There were also times when that drum fill section went wrong. I would of course be keeping in mind where the beat is, but Paul would sometimes come in on the off-beat, and this happened on other songs too. Fortunately Bruce and I used to stay together most of the time, but occasionally Bruce would switch to the beat that Paul was on, so I would have to make a quick adjustment and it wasn't always seamless. It's a bit like marching, then all of a sudden having to change step very quickly to keep up. But then there were times when Paul would twig he had come in on the off-beat and so change, but by then I had changed and then we would all be equally out of sync. The version of 'Tube Station' on *Dig The New Breed* is a good example of shifting to the off-beat because that's where Paul came in.

'Down In The Tube Station' was released in October and reached number 15 in the charts. We didn't have a B-side in mind until the news filtered through about the death of Keith Moon. We talked among ourselves and came up with the idea of recording a version of the Who song 'So Sad About Us' from their second album. This wasn't a song we had in our box of covers; we just learnt it specially. In many ways the song was very different to what The Who were producing around that mid-sixties period. We all liked it for the lyric 'so sad about us' and we saw it as a fitting tribute to Moon. I was as stunned by the news of his death as the next person but I guess I always thought it was an inevitable outcome for Moonie, something many thought would happen to him one day. He was on that self-destruct path, like many others from those heady rock'n'roll days.

Of course I admired Keith Moon as a drummer even though he wasn't really my sort of drummer. His drumming was like his life, close to the edge. I had a conversation once with the managing director of Premier Drums, Roger Horrobin. During Moonie's drumming life with The Who, Premier supplied many kits to him. He told me that there would be boxes of drums sitting on the side of the stage, ready to replace those that Moonie would break throughout a show. He told me that Moonie would do the most outrageous things on stage, like going for a drum fill and those looking on would think to themselves that he was never going to make it round the drums in time, but he'd go for it anyway. He was like a man sitting in a wheelchair spinning on one wheel – it was as if he could fall over at any time. I think most of Keith Moon's drumming sounded like he was pretty much on the edge and this I liked, as it added tension to things. But discipline wise, I just don't think he planned anything, he simply just went for it; that was the type of character he was. Playing drums is really just an extension of your personality and you can see Moonie's in his playing. I'm just not like that. If I don't think I can pull off a drum fill in the time available, I just avoid trying. That's me. I like to have things well-rehearsed as much as possible and be in control. I try to play within my limits, I know not to push it too far because if I do I'll know that you run the risk of falling off. I see it as a scale from one to 10 and if you know your limitations are at nine, then don't push it to 10. It keeps things safe with less chance of making a mistake. Keith Moon was always on 10 and pushing for 11.

Soon after 'Tube Station' came out *All Mod Cons* was released. The title certainly caught people's attention, but like most things where Paul and his lyrics are concerned they were left open for interpretation. *All Mod Cons* meant something for those wandering around in parkas and to others it meant all modern conveniences. Yet, if you look at the album cover, there are no modern conveniences to be seen. The sleeve and title are all about contradictions. On the day of the photo shoot I remember that we hung the guitar and snare drum from the roof using fishing line; and we had to wait for them to stop swinging before the shot could be taken. There was no Photoshop back then so this was the only way we could do it. We did a few poses with jackets on, jackets off, sitting down, standing up; it was a typical photo shoot in that respect. Then once we got the proofs back on huge contact sheets to check and sign off, we liked what we got and that went on to be used on the album cover. Someone will have a stack of Jam contact sheets with pen lines crossed through those where one of us is laughing or has our eyes shut. Going through such contact sheets became another part of the routine of being in The Jam.

Out of all The Jam's album covers my favourite is *Setting Sons*, but I do like all the covers as they all stand out in their own way. There was something left open about the *Setting Sons* cover, and it's not because the band are not featured on it. It was almost an anti-statement, like The Beatles used on their 'White' album, whereas the influence for *Sound Affects* was the BBC 'Effects' albums that were around during that time. I don't know what the individual images were meant to represent, like the baby or the telephone box, maybe they represented just sounds! My least favourite, however, is *The Gift* cover. It reminded me of those fifties record covers that my parents had.

Around the time of *All Mod Cons* my drumming was changing and by this time I was using a Yamaha kit. Chris Parry asked if he could borrow the kit because he was recording The Cure and he needed a kit for the studio he was working in, which was somewhere near Barnes I think. I remember visiting the studio one evening after me and Dickie Bell had been out on the piss. I can't remember why we were even in Barnes but it wasn't because we were going to see Chris. I remember I ended up putting my foot through a window in the studio, and a great shard of glass went through my ankle. There was blood everywhere. God knows what the members of The Cure were thinking but they were probably pleased when I was taken away to the hospital. Since then I've had no feeling in my big toe; you can tread on it now and I wouldn't even know.

For some reason I never ever really liked that Yamaha kit much. It used to feed back a lot in the monitors and rumble, so there were always constant humming noises coming from it that bothered me. As a result I returned to using Premier drums. The drum shells were much thicker and I preferred their robustness; also Premier offered me a great deal at the time and I got freebie drum kits. I built up a good relationship with Premier and this meant they actually even made a personalised drum kit for me. I gave them some specifics and suggestions. For example, I wanted some long toms made. At first I only wanted the two high toms but I wasn't sure what size would work best, so I asked for three different sizes with the intention of only using two but when the three turned up I liked them all and thought, 'Oh bollocks, I'll just use all three then,' so I did and that became the 'Great White' kit.

Premier also gave me a snare drum that was very much a copy of a Ludwig. It was a 6½" by 14" steel shell drum. I love steel snare drums and have never much liked wooden ones. In recent years I have used a Black Beauty Ludwig snare, which even when I bought it cost a lot of money. I've been carrying that snare around for a few years. I've got a few old Jam drums and bits of percussion from those days left. I've still got and use the same cow bell that I originally used on '"A" Bomb In Wardour Street' too.

Even though I preferred to use the Ludwig snare, Premier thankfully didn't mind. I also put aside the pedal they gave me in favour of a Speed King pedal, which was fair enough because it wasn't like anybody would be able to see it from out front. Years later when I started The Gift I contacted Premier to tell them about the band, thinking that the original endorsement deal was still in place. I explained to Premier that I needed a new kit. However, Premier had been bought out and the company was a very different beast altogether. I didn't know any one there any more. The person I would deal with kept passing me around and putting me on hold. I felt like I was being fobbed off so I decided to look elsewhere. I fancied the idea of a Ludwig drum kit and contacted them. I explained that I was looking for an endorsement deal and they immediately said 'Yep, no problem'. They took the measurements of the drums that I wanted and although I had to wait a few months, my new drum kit was shipped over from the States. So thank you very much Ludwig drums. What's more I love the kit, it's the best drum kit I've ever owned; nothing ever goes wrong with it, nothing ever breaks, it's so well made, it has a beautiful finish and it's totally reliable. Later I did a few interviews with some drumming magazines to promote the band and sent copies with photos of me behind the kit to that fella at Premier.

It was around the time of *All Mod Cons* that I noticed that Paul, Bruce and I were not spending so much time socialising together. The thing was we already spent so much time together, either on the road or in the studio. On the road and after a show we would head back to the hotel where we would tuck in to the sandwiches organised by John and have a drink. The usual faces – Kenny Wheeler, Dicky Bell, the crew members – would be there. These gatherings often involved much alcohol and John would often have to usher Paul away to his room. Paul was the worst of us for getting up in the morning. More often than not we would be down on the coach, waiting for Paul to appear. There was always a sense of urgency too, because we would have to be on the road as soon as possible, just to ensure we got to the next town in time. Usually soundchecks would be at four o'clock, then we had to check into a hotel, then it was time to get ready for the show itself. It was a common sight in the mornings to see Paul in just his overcoat holding his suitcase that he had just slammed shut with bits of shirt hanging out of it as he hurried to the coach.

I always knew when I'd had enough drinking and after-partying. For me there was always tomorrow but Paul wouldn't be like that, Paul was in the 'now'. And so, there was a lot of sobering on the coach; people sleeping, snoring and sobering up from the night before. But soon there was the familiar hiss of beer bottles opening about lunchtime, usually the leftovers from the night before.

Playing cards was another favoured pastime on the tour coach. John especially liked this and there was always a decent stash of cash on the table. I only ever sat in once and lost my stake instantly. Poker wasn't for me, I couldn't understand it and besides I didn't have a lot of money to play with… or lose for that matter. Plenty of the crew members did though, and this was how the hours were spent on many of those coach trips.

It's incredible to think how much goes into that hour and a half show in the evening. Everything from the time we opened our eyes in the morning was focussed on that hour and a half in the evening. The truth is that most of the day is boring. Killing time was a daily challenge, but it was all part of the job and this we understood and dealt with in our own individual ways.

When we weren't on the road or in the studio we would all head back to our respective homes and we deliberately wouldn't hang out with each other. In many ways this was a much needed period of respite from each other and what we were doing as our jobs. It was nice to reconnect to our own personal lives and families and friends. At the time of *All Mod Cons* I was still at my parents' house; I hadn't yet moved out to Croydon. I didn't really have any hobbies. I would unwind down the pub with my friends, but only in the evenings. I have never been into day-time drinking, I really don't like doing that. I would never get drunk before I had to play a show. This wasn't the case for Paul or Bruce. Paul would start drinking as soon as he could. I certainly recall times in the early days where Paul would be chucking up beside the stage before we went on, sometimes though nerves but sometimes because of drink.

The Jam would have a rider waiting for us at the venues and for this I would have two bottles of red wine, usually Bull's Blood when available, Paul would have two bottles of vodka and Bruce would have two bottles of Bacardi. We didn't always get through it all and I would often take home my bottles of wine. I had stacks of the stuff piled up at home. I remember one year I bought Bruce a birthday present, and not thinking it through properly I got him a bottle of Bacardi. I took it round to his house and handed it to him and his face was a picture, he then opened up one of the cupboards in his kitchen and showed me that it was full of unopened Bacardi bottles.

The other thing about being on the road is that eating isn't always the healthiest. We did, however, learn things fairly early on and stopped eating at service stations, though there's probably not a service station in the whole of the UK that I have not eaten in. It was also getting more difficult because whenever we stopped at a service station people would recognise us and want to spend time with us, which was fine and we never complained but all we wanted to do was have some food before carrying on with our journey. As an alternative we would often pull off the road when we spotted a pub that looked OK for food. But this had its own problems, sometimes because back then not all pubs liked coaches turning up. I suppose the trade from travelling football fans or working men's clubs' 'days out' were more hassle than they were worth. Nowadays, these types of establishments would kill to get such a coachload in.

There was one occasion where we pulled over and started to pile into this roadside pub. The woman behind the bar screamed, 'You can't come in here, you're a coachload,' but there were only about eight of us. We tried to explain that we just wanted some grub but she wasn't having any of it and kicked us out and then she started locking all the doors and windows behind us. We weren't very happy with this so we all lined up outside her front door and pissed against her windows to protest.

Eating just before a gig made us lethargic and this made playing an energetic show difficult. So we would always try to eat just after the four o'clock soundcheck. This would usually give us five hours to digest it before we went on at around nine. The other thing about the emerging daily timings was that the hotels we stayed at often served as practical gathering points for our press meetings. The hotel foyers especially became the focal point for every meeting on arrival, departure and of all sorts of things. We spent a lot of time hanging around in hotel foyers.

When I did go back to home to Woking I had it fairly easy. I think it was the same for Bruce, but it was very different for Paul. By the time of *Setting Sons* Paul had moved out of Woking and was renting a ground-floor flat in Pimlico. He would sometimes have some hassle from fans who had found out where he lived. Frequently he would have to be dropped off round the corner so he could slip into his flat undetected. Back then Kenny drove Paul around a lot because Paul didn't have a driving licence. For some London shows both Bruce and I would drive to the venue in our own cars. It was easier for us and life in The Jam was never about limos.

I did feel sorry for Paul because he had bars fitted on the windows of his flat. I wouldn't have been able to live like that; it would have been like living in a little prison for me. Paul had chosen to live in London because he loved the lifestyle usually associated with London and wanted to live with that kind of image. Plus there were more and more fans turning up on John and Ann's doorstep asking if Paul was home. And to their credit they would often let the fans in to have a cup of tea, but this soon became a problem. There was one occasion when a multitude of mods with their scooters turned up and parked outside the Wellers' council house. That must have got the neighbours wondering what the hell was going on, and there were several complaints.

But the rent on the flat cost Paul a fortune, which was stupid especially as he would sometimes make fun of me because I was in the process of buying my own place. Having a mortgage was all a bit too establishment for Paul. The real joke was that he was paying twice as much on his rent than I was for my mortgage. Paul would do strange things like that. I remember him telling me once that he refused to have a patterned carpet and instead just have a plain black one. The thing was that the plain black carpet was more expensive than patterned. Another time he refused to buy a stereo because he loved his Dansette Major and thought there was something wrong about people that listened to their music through stereos. Paul had a rebel spirit but sometimes what he did or thought just didn't seem to make sense.

The opening track on *Setting Sons* is 'Girl On The Phone', which related to some of those 'stalker' experiences that Paul had to endure and it was something that he had to come to terms with. But he did get fed up with it. Who wouldn't? We loved the fans and we were grateful for them but sometimes they did get in the way of our own private hells… I mean lives. We kind of expected it at the venues and sometimes after shows we wouldn't be able to get out of the building because all the external doors would be crammed with fans blocking the way. Simply running from one exit to another to try and find a way out was not always very successful. Many times Tim Parsons, the tour promoter, would explain the situation and offer a solution. He owned a fast Ford Capri at the time. Tim arranged for the coach to pull up outside one of the exit doors and of course the word got around and the fans raced to find it. In that small window of opportunity that had opened up Tim would drive up in his Capri to the door where we would be waiting and hiding and we would make a dash for the car, squeeze in and spin off like a scene from *Starsky & Hutch*, and all before the fans waiting by the coach had realised that they had been tricked. The coach driver had a lot of fun smiling at the poor fans before he would slip it into gear and casually pull away – with no Jam members inside. Venues like the Rainbow were terrible for this. We just wanted to get home or get to the hotel bar.

There was one night when I was recording some percussion in

the Townhouse studios in Shepherd's Bush, alone with Vic Smith, everyone else had gone home. There was a pub opposite and a bunch of mods were having a drink in there. The pub attracted a lot of mods because they knew there would be a chance that The Jam may be in the studio across the road or in the area. On this occasion they burst into the studios and were rushing around all the corridors and diving in and out of rooms. Other than Vic and me the place was empty. Vic went out to calm them down and I hid behind one of the thick studio doors. I could hear them shouting, 'Where's The Jam, where's Paul, where's Rick, where's Bruce' and Vic was trying to tell them that none were in. I can still hear the sound now of one lad telling Vic to pass on the message, 'Tell Rick to come and have a drink with us over in the pub.'

Vic had quite a bit of convincing to do until they eventually calmed down, listened to what he had to say and left. It wasn't scary stuff and it didn't happen that often but it could be intimidating and unfortunately, for Paul, it was him that had to deal with most of this sort of behaviour. People and fans didn't always realise that it wasn't just our work places that got invaded it was our lives too. Thankfully nothing too serious ever happened and mostly it was all just good fun and truth be said, a bit of a game.

And credit to the fans – they had ingenious ways of finding things out, our phone numbers, where we lived and our secret gigs like the ones we did under the names John's Boys or The Eton Rifles. I used to think we had a mole in the band camp!

CHAPTER SIX

1979 started with the usual rehearsals, now at Nomis Studios which was located within a studio and office complex in Sinclair Road in Shepherd's Bush, and owned by Simon Napier Bell who'd managed a few big acts over the years. Nomis was Simon spelt backwards. It was a large building with a selection of rehearsal rooms, and an area at the rear that served as access for the trucks and equipment that was stored there. Nomis had really good facilities, which suited us. We used the yard to film some of the 'Absolute Beginners' video, the one where we are jumping through the smoke.

The Jam also had offices in the building, as did other bands' managements, which meant that there were always loads of people coming and going. It was mostly only John Weller and Kenny Wheeler who set up camp, holding meetings with the tour managers and the crew. Paul, Bruce and I occasionally went in for meetings, if and when we had things to discuss. When we were on the road or in the studio, meetings were in the bar of whatever hotel we were staying at or the nearest pub. There were times when John would stroll into the rehearsal room because something had come up, and we would put down our instruments and have a meeting on the spot.

Due to Nomis being so large we had space to keep all our equipment there. I don't think the rent was cheap, but it worked for us as we were able to rehearse, store our gear safely and also have our office. I think John kept hold of that office even after The Jam split up. It may have even been used as the Style Council headquarters for a while.

A new single, 'Strange Town', was due to be released in March, but before that a European tour was organised. As a warm-up, we played Reading University on February 16. Four days later we were in Germany, opening up the tour at The Metropole in Berlin. We passed through Germany, playing in Hamburg then moved onto France where we played at the Stadium in Paris, then onto Rennes, Lyon and Marseille. By now the quality of our hotels and travelling arrangements was improving. Up until this point, room sharing had been a necessity, me sharing with Bruce, Paul with Gill and John with the tour manager (whoever that was at any particular time) but there was a little more money now and although the shows were smaller in Europe to start with, compared to the UK we could afford our own hotel rooms.

We still had to work hard to gain ground with those audiences. It was clear that it was going to take time to build a fanbase in Europe but this was OK because back in the UK the band were doing well, selling records and playing bigger venues to larger crowds. We accepted that we couldn't be big everywhere, all at the same time.

Playing in smaller venues and to smaller crowds didn't affect the way we went about things. We didn't need to adjust our playing or adapt our performances according to size. However, I did look forward to returning to playing live in the UK and the audience that we were building. By 1979 we had established ourselves back at home. I certainly felt more at home playing to British audiences. The European tours were still good and great fun to do, though I never really felt that we went down that well in Germany. When you check The Jam gigging history we didn't play that much there. What I do remember was that there was still a lot of heavy metal interest in Germany, so maybe The Jam just wasn't that appealing to them. As a result I think we were pushed to touring in places that were more receptive. For example we always went down well in Canada. I think Canada was also our second biggest market for record sales. Japan seemed to work too. And it was usual for bands that were touring the States to stop by Japan on their way home.

'That's Entertainment' was released in Germany as a single, maybe as an attempt by Polydor to break into that market. It was pressed and produced there, and so when it appeared in the UK it was as an import. Record companies often work in ways that at first glance seem odd, often tying a release in with a tour or something because it doesn't always make sense releasing in all areas at the same time, and this often results in product being packaged differently or having an alternative track listing.

I think with 'That's Entertainment' someone saw an opportunity and decided to buy up a massive bulk of the 7" singles and simply import them into the UK. It wasn't a UK release and therefore it wasn't allowed to enter the charts. All the same 'That's Entertainment' sold really well in the UK and in Germany too as a local release.

I ran into Barry Cain, a journalist who was involved with *Flexipop*, recently at a club in London. He reminded me that he travelled to Germany with The Jam, and we found ourselves remembering our visit to a prisoner of war camp while we were there. If I remember correctly it was Dachau in Bavaria where a memorial site was founded in 1965 through the initiative of survivors of the concentration camp. It wasn't a planned visit. I think the coach driver saw a sign and shouted out, 'Does anyone want to visit it?' At the time I was unaware of the camp's history or purpose but my memories of visiting that camp have remained with me ever since. Up until then I had only seen stuff on the TV or read about the horrors that people experienced in them. One of the things that left a deep impression on me was that many of the brick buildings had been left standing, whereas the wooden huts had been burned to the ground, partly to kill off any diseases that lurked in them. There was also a crematorium but we weren't allowed to go inside it, only to stand at the entrance and peer in. The room looked cold and empty, but it stirred the imagination. Beside the entrance was a photograph, taken from the exact spot where I stood, that captured a moment when the chamber was packed full of those poor souls who'd been worked to death. The photo showed the dead bodies piled up on top of each other, and it filled me with horror then and still does today. Visiting that place was a stark reminder of how real the concentration camps were and how many innocent lives were lost.

While we were there we also visited one of the sergeant's messes. There were huge boards displaying more photographs of sites around the camp during the Second World War, including images of Hitler and his generals and soldiers marching around. But what struck me was the way that every face on every Nazi had been scratched off by people visiting the camp. It was an impressive statement that chilled me to the bone. It showed me the anger that some still felt towards what had happened, even 30 years after the camp had been closed down. I felt pleased that these camps had not been destroyed completely because they served to remind the world about something that shouldn't be forgotten. During Paul's Style Council years he wrote a song called 'Ghosts Of Dachau'. Maybe our initial trip left such an impact on Paul too that it moved him to write that song a few years after.

It certainly wasn't all morbid being in Germany. I spent plenty of time in their bars too, and in one, after much drinking, I was challenged to a bet. There were a few of us, along with members of the crew, all sat around a table in the beer garden. It fascinated us that the beer was served in steins, which held about two pints. I took on the bet that I could drink a stein in less than one minute. Being already drunk, I stupidly rose to the occasion and achieved the goal with a brief grin of delight. One second later it all come back up in more than record time; an impressive projectile vomiting act that raised a cheer from the locals. Being on the road seemed to provide us with ample opportunities to do silly things. I certainly wouldn't have attempted that stein if I had been sober.

On a day off, a dead day as we called them, still in Germany, a few of us arranged an excursion to a bar in the town where we were playing. We found a nice place with nice bar staff that allowed us to run up what turned into a substantial tab. I think the crew had arrived in the town the night before and already discovered the bar and befriended the bar staff. The crew would often arrive a day earlier than the band because they would travel overnight straight from the previous gig.

For some unknown reason we had taken to drinking champagne cocktails, which didn't come cheap but they tasted nice and did the job. The evening had unfolded nicely and everyone was in good spirits. Satisfied, we decided to head back to the hotel. Dave Liddle trotted off to the toilet. Dave was often on the wrong end of a joke and the rest of us scarpered out of the bar, on our way out telling the bar staff that 'the fat man with the beard' had the money to pay for the drinks. After he had relieved himself and returned to the bar he discovered us all gone and his exit barred. He had no choice but to pick up the tab. When he got back to the hotel he was not in a good mood. We let him suffer for a bit before having a whip round.

Alongside getting pissed and finding ways to amuse ourselves, the sport of choice on tour was usually playing cards for money. It was a good way to kill time on the bus and waiting around in hotels. There were often bundles of cash sitting around, John often carrying a decent wad of it. Bands did back then and there were times when they would get targeted by thieves who had worked this out. It wouldn't take much of a criminal mind to work out that a manager would at some point be leaving a venue after the band's performance carrying a suitcase full of pound notes. I don't think it ever happened to The Jam but I heard stories about other bands getting turned over in this way.

There was one time when some of our Jam money fell foul of some unsavoury person. We had just started a tour in the States. The crew boss for that tour held the cash for settling expenses and paying the crew wages for the coming week. We were in Los Angeles and it was our first day there. He had pulled some dodgy bird and had taken her back to his hotel room, but when he awoke he discovered the bird had gone, along with all the money that he was responsible for. Whoever she was she had cleared him out, leaving him with not as much as a single dollar bill. Of course, John found out and the crew boss was summoned. He took a hell of a bollocking, was put on a plane and told to fuck off back to England.

CHAPTER SEVEN

Life on the road certainly presented many challenges and there are countless stories, and on the whole I was enjoying travelling and touring. The initial excitement of doing *Top Of The Pops* soon wore off and it became a really boring thing to do. Unfortunately it was the only TV programme worth doing at the time in the UK, so it had to be done. It was broadcast once a week and run in a time-honoured manner by traditional BBC types, who were mostly from a different era all together. There was the BBC way of doing things and only the BBC way. It was a very corporate setup and if you wanted to be featured on the show you simply had to comply. The music industry and the BBC were like oil and water. They just didn't mix well. The sound crew and the cameramen were all competent but they weren't allowed to be left to their own devices. There was always someone directing them on the floor.

A typical day would begin with the meet and greet and being rushed towards an initial rehearsal. This was more for the benefit of the director and cameramen, as it helped them map out in which direction they would need to be swinging around during the actual filming. The *TOTP* studio was made up of several mini stages so the attention had to sweep effortlessly from one stage to the next.

During the actual filming there were *TOTP* employees frantically ushering the people in the audience around the cameras and from stage to stage. The audiences always appeared to be bigger than they were when the show was broadcast but at the time of filming there weren't that many really. While the filming was happening, all the bands appearing on the show would have to wait patiently for their turn. It's a similar setup to the way Jools Holland does his show. The difference was that on *TOTP* there were more neon lights flashing, Pan's People or Legs & Co (as they became) were dancing around and a DJ like Mike Reid introduced the acts. The BBC clung very closely to their schedules which meant everything was run in military fashion. Everything had a time allocation, especially the tea breaks.

During rehearsal the playback was always too quiet, so as not to drown out the direction via the cameramen's headphones. This meant that the band could hardly hear anything which made it really difficult to mime along to. The sound rehearsal was followed by a second rehearsal where we had to dress in the clothes that we would be wearing during the actual filming. They needed to know exactly what we would be wearing as they hated anything like dogtooth, for example, because that would give viewers visual problems. There was absolutely no branding permitted either, so you couldn't wear a T-shirt with the name of some company on it.

Miming was horrible. I had to use fibreglass cymbals, which were hilarious because they were a bright yellow or red, not that most viewers noticed or even cared. Rubber pads were placed over the drum skins to dampen them down. It would have been louder in a library on a Tuesday afternoon. Paul would sing onto a microphone that had no lead attached and play guitars with no amps.

After the first two run-throughs, a break would be called and everything would stop for an hour. After that there would be more hanging around until the actual show that evening, which would be filmed with all the punters in attendance. The bands never mixed with any of the audience. Once the filming was completed it was very much over and the bands and audience were instructed to clear off. Half the time members of the audience didn't even know or like what bands were on the show. Once they had applied to be on the show they would have to turn up with no idea what acts would be appearing. It was all pot luck. When you look at old *TOTP* footage you can see unamused faces in the audience. I remember looking out and seeing countless faces looking gormlessly back at me. What *TOTP* did have, however, was a viewing audience…

… unlike *The Old Grey Whistle Test* which was a different kettle of fish entirely. This show was filmed in a big industrial looking room with a large backdrop with the name of the show and the image of the light-bulb man kicking a star, and of course it had whispering Bob Harris as the main presenter. He did like his swivel chair. *The Old Grey Whistle Test* was more musically orientated than chart orientated and it went out later at night, so it appealed to a more serious music fan. It was a good show to do, and we did it in 1978, performing '"A" Bomb In Wardour Street', 'In The Street Today' and 'Billy Hunt'. And we could actually play live. We also performed '"A" Bomb' (and 'David Watts') on *Revolver* in the same year. This show was hosted by the comedian Peter Cook.

The other show on which we were allowed to play live was *The Marc Bolan Show*, which we did in 1977, playing 'All Around The World'. That was the show when Bolan introduced us as Jam, and I lost my drumstick up in the air. It wasn't intentional. Fortunately we had almost finished the song. I don't know how it happened but I managed to catch the tip of one of my sticks on something and I lost my grip and up it went. Playing shows like *The Old Grey Whistle Test*, *Revolver* and *The Marc Bolan Show* was very different to playing live to a crowd. It summoned a different kind of nervousness. There was no second take either, so once it was filmed that was it. And I still don't know what happened to that drumstick. Maybe it's still there because I don't remember it coming down.

Generally I adjusted well to whatever setting I found myself in, whether it was playing live in front of 200 people or 2,000 or doing a television show that was potentially being broadcast to a million viewers. In those days the Musicians' Union also had more clout, and one of the things they demanded was that any song that was presented on *TOTP* had to be re-recorded the night before the song was played on the show. So even though bands had a recording of their own, a new recording had to be submitted. Another rule was that anyone who played on that record also had to be on the show. What would happen was that the record company would hire a recording studio on the Tuesday night, after getting the nod that their artist was to be included and get the band in, to record the song again. But some songs took a lot longer than a few hours to record so time was limited. I mean can you imagine a band like Queen trying to re-record a version of 'Bohemian Rhapsody' in a few hours on a Tuesday night? What was more the MU would send a representative down to the studio to make sure the band was actually doing the recording. The band members would be present along with an engineer and producer and the recording would start. But at some point during the evening, someone, usually from the record company, would take the MU rep out to the pub for a pint and a bite to eat and while they were out the tapes would get swapped over, a copy of the original tapes having been sneaked in earlier. This meant by the time the MU returned to collect the tape it was finished and he could leave with the recorded version that the band wanted. It was all a bit of a farce really and I'm sure the MU reps knew what was going on.

The charts in those days were compiled from sales up to and including Saturday after the shops closed. Nowhere was open on Sundays back then so no records could be sold. This meant that Monday was the day that the sales would be collated, on Tuesdays the results were conveyed to the record companies and by the Wednesday *TOTP* would have chosen what acts they wanted on the show and the bands were told, and rehearsals and filming completed so the show could be broadcast on Thursday nights (later moving to Fridays).

Once the record company got the call from the Beeb it was action stations. In the eighties some bands would just send in a video, and this meant that if they were abroad on tour or too busy to leave the studio where they were working they could still have their song appear on the show but not actually have to turn up and suffer the day of filming. The BBC would allow only a small part of *TOTP* content to be videos. If you were number one it was guaranteed that you would be included but for everybody else in the Top 30 appearances were once a fortnight and only if you were rising up the chart. The show was always too short, 30 minutes a week to represent the Top 30?

Up until the nineties really, Britain was starved of any decent music programmes. In the sixties they had *Ready Steady Go!*, in the seventies and eighties it was *TOTP*, and *The Tube* from 1982 until 1987, but it wasn't until the nineties and the arrival of Sky and MTV that things opened up. However, *Top Of The Pops* did mean a great deal to many fans, for years the only TV show that showcased the only chart that mattered. Seeing Boy George on his debut appearance with his band Culture Club was a shocking experience for many, and for days after arguments were raging over whether he was a boy or a girl.

I met Boy George in the BBC bar which was not the easiest place to get into. If you were on a show it was generally OK but it wasn't an open door to everyone, and I don't even remember if Boy George was appearing on the same *TOTP* as The Jam. He may have been there for something else, but we ended up sitting opposite each other and just got talking. What struck me was that he wasn't wearing anything too feminine. Instead he was dressed from head to toe in black. I also remember thinking that he was much taller than I thought, which surprised me.

On another occasion I spotted Graham Fellows, aka Jilted John, and asked him for his autograph. We were both sitting outside on the balcony terrace area and even though I recognised him at first I couldn't place him. Eventually the penny dropped and I went over and started chatting to him. I think 'Gordon Was A Moron' was his hit at the time. He was a lovely guy and very down to earth.

Various DJs were always in and out of the bar too. Some steered clear because they were fed up with being pestered. The bar was always full of characters. Even the security guy that manned the door with his army-style moustache was a character. He took his job very seriously and if you didn't have a pass to get in you simply didn't get in. Thankfully we never had any trouble with him.

'Strange Town' was released on March 17 and two television appearances were arranged to help promote the single and the song got up to number 15. It was about an alien coming to Earth, at least that is the most accepted interpretation that fans have attached to it. The B-side was a song called 'The Butterfly Collector'. In his book *The Jam: A Beat Concerto* Paolo Hewitt wrote that the song was about a club owner but I always remembered it being about predatory girls hanging around to add the 'pop star butterflies' to their collection. Paul's lyrics explain it all really, telling a story about how someone collects fame by being around others. There are always people like that 'hanging around' bands, turning up at press conferences and photo shoots just to be involved. They don't do anything else. Often Paul's lyrics are not that obvious. Take a song like 'The Bitterest Pill', which is about catching a dose of the clap and then having to face up to the girlfriend and explain yourself. That is the bitterest pill that has to be swallowed. Paul was brilliant at drawing on personal experiences either directly or indirectly and translating them into lyrics. It's a brave thing to do. It also meant that it was easier to relate to Paul's songs.

There were some things about the *Beat Concerto* book that annoyed Bruce and me. By the time of the book The Jam were about to split up, and we were told that Paolo was going to do an article about The Jam for a newspaper and it would probably be a centre spread. A meeting was arranged for an interview at what was then Polydor's studio near Hyde Park, which became Solid Bond Studios, between myself, Bruce and Paolo. We spent less than half an hour talking about The Jam and how it was coming to an end. We didn't really contribute as much as we would have liked. Somewhere along the way that article turned into a full-on official

Jam biography, a very one-sided story! Bruce and I never saw any money from it either. Nothing against Paolo; we had known him from the Woking years and I respect his work, but somewhere along the line the goal posts got shifted.

After 'Strange Town' was released speculation was rife at the record company as to whether we would get our first number one record, or even when we would achieve it. Getting a number one record was never our aim. Yes, we understood that there was a great deal of kudos to be had by reaching the top of the pops but it wasn't anything that we lost any sleep over. Of course, there were benefits to having a number one record. It meant automatic radio play, which would help sell records.

I was pleased that getting a number one record wasn't one of The Jam's major goals; neither Paul, Bruce nor I got into the music industry just to get a number one record. There were other things that were of more importance. We just wanted to make great records. The charts were really just some sort of milestone that supposedly reflected how successful a band was. And just because a song was in the charts didn't necessarily mean it was a good song. The charts have been littered with gimmicks and novelty songs and many have reached number one, often keeping a good song off the number one spot. 'The Bitterest Pill' reached number two and was prevented from getting to number one because the top spot was held by Survivor's 'Eye Of The Tiger', a song that became massive because it was used in one of the *Rocky* films.

Also, once a band gets a number one record there's nowhere else to go. There can be a downside to this. And it's not easy to keep on getting number one records. The Jam was very fortunate to have four number ones in all, and we felt fortunate too, but it wasn't always at the front of our minds despite the expectations of the record company to achieve greater sales. A few weeks after 'Strange Town' was released we went on tour, passing through places like Toronto, Chicago, Boston and Detroit. Then in May we returned to the UK and played further gigs in towns such as Sheffield,

Liverpool and Glasgow. Most of May was spent on the road. Our last gig was in Portsmouth on the 24th. Thankfully we only played one show in June, and we got a well-earned break.

In mid-1979 I took up an offer from an old work colleague to share his flat in Croydon. I had met Roy while working in Woking and we had stayed in touch. He now worked on oil rigs and was away for long periods at a time. This meant that if I moved in I would have the place to myself for the most part. I liked the idea and I would also be closer to London. Plus it was time for me to move out of my parents' house now I could afford to do so. I packed everything I owned into the back of my Triumph TR6 and drove the short distance up the A3 to my new home in Bensham Lane, Croydon.

Roy owned the whole of the terrace house and he had decided to convert it into two flats. We hardly ever saw each other because when he was back from the oil rigs, I would be away on tour and when I was back he would be off. I really liked living in Croydon. On the rare occasions when we were both home we would venture out to a fantastic Greek restaurant just around the corner. When we were both home we were always eating out. Cooking meals was a very rare occurrence.

My room was at the back of the upstairs flat and Roy's room was at the front. The downstairs flat was rented by two gay guys. They were always throwing parties and told the most hilarious jokes. Roy, my girlfriend, Lesley, and I would always get an invitation so with the added benefit of not having far to go to get home, we would pop downstairs. Lesley especially loved them; she could always dance her heart out.

There was one occasion when I had to move back to my parents' house because Roy had decided to make some alterations to the flat. I returned home from a tour earlier than Roy expected to find the place in total upheaval. Along the hallway wall I had noticed a pile of heavy duty wooden beams, which it turned out he had got from some nearby building site by simply driving in a lorry and loading it up in broad daylight before driving off unchallenged.

He had decided to knock out some internal walls and change the whole layout of the rooms, including mine, but he'd forgotten to mention anything to me. As I reached the top of the stairs I was confronted by a cloud of dust and Roy emerging with a large sledgehammer. 'What are you doing here? You should be in America!' he said.

I found living in Croydon suited me because I was spending a fair bit of time travelling into London either for rehearsing, recording or playing shows. I felt quite happy buzzing around London in my pride and joy, a burgundy TR6. But I was always back and forth to Woking, to see my mates and parents, spending the evening at the Robin Hood pub. Back in the seventies, no one thought anything of having a couple of pints and driving. Attitudes surrounding drink driving were very different back then.

Although the band was working most of the time and gaining a degree of success, contrary to popular belief, being 'famous' or a 'pop star' did not automatically mean 'wealth'. I didn't have a lot of disposable cash. As a band we paid ourselves a small wage and lived on our hotel bills and per diems. Most of our income was for paying band expenses, such as touring costs and crew wages. Cheap second-hand cars were at the time unreliable machines and I was always running them until they gave up on me. I had old Minis, an Austin A40 and a Morris 1100, which at least had a current MOT, a beaten up MGB that had no second gear, and by the time we released 'David Watts' I had bought an old Volvo 144 from a guy that John Weller knew who sometimes used to drive us to and from the airport. The dark blue Volvo had an impressive service history and a more impressive mileage but despite this it was in excellent condition.

However, one night while I tried to get home from the BBC studios in White City it lost a fan belt and several bolts. I tried in vain to fix it but soon gave up. I had no money in my pocket and was covered in oil, so I had no choice but to walk back to the BBC studios to try and catch a lift from John if I hadn't already missed him. Luckily as I walked into the front entrance John was just leaving. When I explained my predicament I could hear comments from others who were leaving: 'What's the drummer in a top band doing in an old banger anyway?' It was decided that it would be fair to draw some money from the band's bank account. Paul, Bruce and I were each allotted £2,000. Two grand was a lot of money in 1979, more than I needed to spend on a new car. The deposit I put down on my first house in 1980 was £2,000.

I had my eye on a Cherokee jeep that I had seen in a showroom at the end of the Goldhawk Road, near to Townhouse Studios, where we were doing some recording. It was a beast of a machine. I had been passing it for weeks and was always glancing over, but on the day I went down to the showroom with the cash in my hand it was gone, sold already. I was absolutely gutted. Being determined to buy a car that day I looked around the showroom and spotted a blue Cadillac Seville, so I went home in that instead.

A few weeks later I decided that I didn't like the blue so had it sprayed, Ford diamond white. I loved it. It was a great car but the six-litre V8 drank fuel like there was no tomorrow, something like six miles to the gallon. The strange thing was, I discovered that when it was brand new it had been imported from Canada to Old Woking, to a body shop right opposite where I worked soon after leaving school. The Cadillac had been sent there to be converted to a right hand drive. It's quite possible that I may have even seen the car sitting on the forecourt all those years earlier.

I kept the Cadillac for a few years but eventually it was left at the bottom of my garden when I moved house to Sunningdale. I didn't drive it much and over one winter it sank into the ground (right up to the exhaust pipe). I even found mice living in it. I never got to drive it again. In fact while it was slowly rotting in my garden some guy knocked on my front door one afternoon and offered to buy it from me. I told him about the car's condition but he was certain that he wanted it. On the day he came to collect it the engine started up with no problems (which surprised me). He handed me a wad of cash and drove it away, along with a General Motors manual I had picked up in America. However, he returned about a week later asking for his money back because he had discovered there were problems with the engine. But it was sold as seen and I didn't give him his money back; after all the rest of the car was OK and he even got some mice out of it.

CHAPTER EIGHT

On our next USA tour John was approached by an American manager and a deal was done for co-management in the States. It was felt that we could gain more coverage if we supported larger acts in larger venues, and we were booked into places like the Tower Theatre in Philadelphia and the Palladium in New York. Some of the venues we had played the previous year when we supported the Blue Öyster Cult and Be Bop Deluxe. The Blue Öyster Cult tour had been hard. The audience knew nothing about us and just didn't understand us at all. There was one guy at one of the Be Bop Deluxe shows wearing a black suit and tie, white shirt; he was enjoying it and was standing up and dancing about. The security forced him to stay in his seat. If the gig was a 'seated venue' that was what you were expected to do; there was no pushing and shoving near the stage like we were used to back home.

It's never easy for support acts. Some acts that supported The Jam had it tough. Bananarama supported us at a gig at the Michael Sobell Sports Centre in London. They weren't scheduled to be on the bill and somehow got included but it hadn't been that well thought out. They had no band just a backing track and three microphones, and they only performed a short set, a handful of songs. It wasn't exactly what Jam fans expected or even wanted and there was an atmosphere of 'what the fuck is this all about' but I think Bananarama just about held their own.

The support acts that I mostly recall were New Hearts (who became Secret Affair), Apocalypse (which featured writer Tony Fletcher), The Piranhas and The Dolly Mixtures whom I liked. I found them to be quite amusing, like a more streetwise Bananarama with their hobnail boots and floral dresses. And they were always going off to the sweet shop to buy sweets. I didn't always get to see the support acts, though, because we would be getting ready backstage.

The thing about American audiences was that they really behaved themselves. The Japanese were very polite too. They were fabulous people but we did find it very different to the gigs in Britain. Their culture at shows was completely different. For instance, the shows always started early so that the young people could get home at a reasonable time. By nine o'clock we were heading back to the hotel.

It was the autograph hunters that used to make me laugh because when you flicked through their books you could see all the other names that they had collected. And the range of artists and various genres of music was astounding. There would be signatures from members from ska, new wave and heavy metal bands. The Japanese were just music fans and didn't indulge themselves in the type of tribalism that we had back in the UK.

I do remember two Japanese fans; both girls, one named Keiko who even moved to the UK to be near to The Jam and follow us around for a while. The pair of them obviously stood out. John was very aware of the loyal Jam fans. One time a group of fans followed us to the States but as we moved across the country, covering great distances, the group of fans was shrinking in number because one by one they were running out of money. By the time we reached Los Angeles only two of the group remained but they were short of cash too and couldn't even afford the flight back to the UK. We paid for their tickets home.

There were many times when Bruce and I had Jam fans sleeping at the bottom of our beds in some hotel room because they couldn't afford a room of their own. Some of the fans would turn up at as many shows as they could, and we often wondered how they could afford it at all.

After doing some interviews in Phoenix we had the evening off so I decided to go for a walk and find a deli. I wanted to get some food and drink to take back to the hotel because it was cheaper to buy food in the delis than it was in the hotels. I didn't know where the shops were but headed off in the most likely direction. I eventually found a deli and selected my food and some beers and placed them on the shop's counter. There was a middle-aged couple that ran the place and asked me for some ID because proof of age was a big thing in the States. The only official ID I had on me was my British driving licence which I handed over to the man. I then spent the next 10 minutes trying to explain to him how the date of birth was written on a UK driving licence. He got really excited and called out to his wife, telling her that she needed to come and see 'some Brit's driving licence' and how we write our dates. It took them a while to 'get it'.

It was early evening by this time and still hot and dry for the walk back. I suppose I must have been doing something unusual or suspicious because a police car pulled up beside me and demanded that I stop. The officer questioned me. He wanted to know where I had been, where I was headed, who I was and asked for some ID. So, again I had to explain the British driving licence and he was fascinated as he had never seen a British driving licence before.

On some 'dead days' on tour I would just decide to leave the hotel and go exploring. Sometimes I would find myself in awkward situations which would only be made worse if you couldn't speak their language. What I would do was carry a complimentary book of matches that most hotels supplied, and they always had the hotel's address written on them. I often found myself fishing around in my pocket – hoping that I had discarded the matches from the previous day's hotel – to show a taxi driver where I needed to go. One night I was showing the taxi driver the matchbook and he blankly refused to take me to the hotel on the box, which was fair enough as it turned out to be a few hundred miles away in Ontario. I was in Detroit at the time. Well it was late and I may have had a beer or two.

Hotels in warmer places like California could be good fun, especially the Sunset Marquis. It was a typical hotel like you see in the movies; a large pool surrounded by chalets. Throughout the sixties and seventies many a band had thrown beds and TVs from their chalet windows into those pools but The Jam weren't like that. We never saw the point, especially as we knew that covering any costs would come out of our wages and this we weren't prepared to do. It seemed 'old hat', just to get a bit of extra media attention.

There were a few embarrassing incidents. One time beside a pool in Los Angeles, Alan Belcher grabbed hold of me and jumped into the pool. Up until that point I had been quite content resting on a sun bed, sipping a cold beer and killing time. I splashed about for a bit, much to everyone's laughter and Alan swam to the edge and got out. What Alan and the observers didn't know was that I wasn't a great swimmer and I wasn't splashing about for fun. They continued to laugh as I continued to bob up and down. Eventually someone realised that I wasn't pranking about and yelled out, 'I don't think he can swim.' This alerted Alan and he quickly jumped back in and pulled me to the side. As a result of this incident I spent the next few days teaching myself how to swim and I managed to perfect my doggy paddle style.

The Hyatt House, or the Riot House as it became lovingly known, was on Sunset Boulevard. It was fairly near the Whisky A Go Go so bands since the sixties who played there had stayed at the hotel. The walls and hallways of the Hyatt have many stories to tell; indeed it was reported that John Bonham once rode a motorcycle through those very hallways, both Keith Moon and Keith Richards threw televisions out of their windows and Jim Morrison, who was living at the hotel at the time, got kicked out

'Absolute Beginners' photo shoot, 1981. DEREK D'SOUZA

On stage at the Greyhound, Fulham. BILL AXE

Greyhound, 175 Fulham Palace Road, where admission was often free, Saturday March 20, 1976. BILL AXE

Trans Global Express tour. NEIL 'TWINK' TINNING

Rick on the tour bus. RICK BUCKLER ARCHIVES

The Japanese audience loved us wearing the Divine Wind headband on stage. RICK BUCKLER ARCHIVES

remier Drums made these custom size toms for me but the extra long shells were difficult to manufacture. DEREK D'SOUZA

rans Global Express tour. DEREK D'SOUZA

An enlarged Jam take a break during rehearsals for their last appearance on *The Tube*, 1982. With Caron Wheeler, Claudie Fontaine and Jim Telford. ITV/REX FEATURES

The Tube, 1982. ITV/REX FEATURES

Backstage at the Michael Sobell Sports Centre, Islington, December 13, 1981. NEIL 'TWINK' TINNING

On their last tour The Jam's farewell was supposed to be five sold-out gigs at the Wembley Arena but then a final date at Brighton was added for December 11, 1982. RICK BUCKLER ARCHIVES

for dangling by his fingertips from his window. The hotel has since been featured in several films. By comparison I enjoyed a relatively peaceful time staying there with The Jam.

In November 1979 The Jam were featured on the front cover of *NME* again. This was always a massive milestone for us and for me personally. In the seventies *NME*, along with *Sounds* and *Melody Maker*, was a really important paper for music lovers. To be included in those pages was considered to be really top dog stuff. And then to actually be on the front cover was very special. Seeing the band on the front really felt to me like we had truly arrived back in 1977. Our first cover was in April, 1977.

That 1979 edition of *NME* came out at the same time as our new single 'The Eton Rifles' (David Cameron's favourite record apparently) was released. This was our third single of the year and it reached number three in the chart, our highest position to date. We felt that there had been a shift in the band's popularity. It was in this same week that we also played two gigs calling ourselves John's Boys and The Eton Rifles. Then, three weeks later *Setting Sons* was released, becoming our best-selling album to date.

We recorded *Setting Sons* at Townhouse Studios in Goldhawk Road. Making that album was an intense business, as we concentrated a lot more on the sound and the arrangements of the songs, and we seemed to do many more takes than we were used to. By the end of the recordings, there were boxes of tapes around the wall of the control room. It was generally a different process doing that album from what had gone before, and like all of our albums it didn't sound like the one that preceded it.

Vic Coppersmith-Heaven seemed to spend more time with overdubbing and adding things like percussion, guitar parts and backing vocals. More time was spent refining parts than we had done previously. I think we all got on really well recording in Townhouse Studios and this contributed to the end product. There was more going on within the tracks on the album, which made them sound fuller. Some songs like 'Little Boy Soldiers' couldn't be compared to anything that we had done before.

With *Setting Sons* each time you listen to a song you hear something new or forgotten in it. Every song was full of little details that had been missed with earlier listening. 'Thick As Thieves', 'Private Hell' and 'Wasteland' are all great songs. We recorded 'Heat Wave' live in the studio and kept it for the album. The recording captured that raw energy that can only be achieved when all the band members are playing live together. We knew the song well and we liked it. Originally recorded by Martha Reeves & The Vandellas, The Who had recorded a version of it and included it on *A Quick One,* the same album that had 'So Sad About Us' on it. It was great to do even though it went against the way all the other songs on the album had been recorded.

I have often been asked whether a certain song from this Jam album or that Jam album is a particular favourite. I find this always a very difficult question to answer. The truth is I loved doing them all. Some songs stand out for different reasons but it doesn't mean I favour them over others. 'Girl On The Phone' I liked for all sorts of reasons. I especially liked Paul's lyrics on that song. The production is really good with the way the song ends with the phone ringing off and the girl's voice can be heard. That voice belonged to the girl who worked in the reception at Townhouse. We literally asked her to speak into the internal phone between the reception and the studio.

But if someone asks me next week what's a particular favourite on *Setting Sons* my memory about doing a certain song may offer up something different. 'Burning Sky' on the other hand I found to be quite difficult to record. There were some really complicated parts in it. There are different drum parts for all the different sections of the song. I had to really concentrate to play that song and when I had the arrangement set, I stuck to it, strictly.

'Smithers-Jones' was the last song that Bruce contributed to a Jam album. It was about his dad, not necessarily directly, but I think Bruce drew some inspiration from what his dad experienced. His dad worked for Charrington's, a coal distribution company. I think the story was that he found himself unemployed one day and thought, 'Well I might as well retire then now.' There was that sense of a golden handshake and thanks very much but you're not needed any more so 'see ya'.

Setting Sons was the album where Bruce and I spent more time than we usually did going into the studio of an evening and really rehearsing. This meant that when we all got together in the studio the next day to actually record the song we were already well-rehearsed. Bruce and I wanted to feel confident by the time of the actual recording. There's nothing worse than having to record a song but having to hold back because you don't feel totally confident about your part. We had done this to a certain extent on earlier albums, and that was fine for then and for those songs but by *Setting Sons* we were aiming to achieve something better. In the studio the drums are always the foundation on which the rest of a song is built, so the drum parts have to be recorded right. After that and once the guitars and vocals are added there's no turning back. So it simply has to be right from the start.

Much has been said about the album's title. There is a sense of the sun setting on the nation's empire or that England is a nation fit for heroes, and that kind of feel runs within the album. The cover used a photograph by Andrew Douglas of a small bronze sculpture by Benjamin Clemens that he produced in 1919 called *The St. John's Ambulance Bearers*. It was a choice that very much reflected the content of the songs on the album. Sadly, that bronze sculpture has been in long-term storage for many years, so nobody has been able to see it for a long time.

When *Setting Sons* was released in 1979 the memory of the Second World War was still very much alive. There were still plenty of people around who had fought or grown up during the war years. It wasn't a distant memory for them. The notion of *Setting Sons* being some kind of concept album is quite loose and that certainly wasn't in our minds while we were recording it. It most definitely wasn't an attempt to be The Jam's *Tommy* or *The Wall*. All Jam songs – and Paul's lyrics – are open to any interpretation from whoever is listening, and it's the same with whatever is delivered visually. The British bulldog, Union Jack and Army helmet all mean different things to different people but in many ways they are of a kind, and this is what has made Jam songs work for so many people across so many generations. Jam songs just don't have a singular monochrome idea, they are much broader. It just so happened that when *Setting Sons* was released in 1979 it was exactly 40 years after the outbreak of the Second World War.

CHAPTER NINE

It was on one of our trips to LA that another 'funny at the time' incident occurred, only this time it was John Weller who provided the entertainment. The band, John and some of the crew had some time to kill so we went for a drink. We found a typical LA bar that was especially dark and dingy, with a dollop of seediness thrown in for good measure too. Walking in off the sunlit street into those bars was always a strange experience. I found them very moody.

We entered and made a beeline for the bar to order our drinks. I guess John must have been a little exhausted because when we slotted ourselves into gaps at the bar he made for what he presumed was a vacant stool and plonked himself down on it. Only the stool wasn't vacant and this massive black guy leaped up with surprise, not having expected someone attempting to sit on his lap. John was naturally shocked and apologetic as he hurriedly backed away to rejoin the rest of us.

Touring provided many opportunities to have a laugh; usually at someone else's expense. There was always this notion – a mantra even – that whatever happens on tour stays on tour, and this ruling applied to everyone. I think it was Paul who actually took the lead on this particular prank, but a corset was found in someone's hotel room. We thought it would be funny to hide it in John's suitcase, which we somehow managed to do on the last day of the tour without John realising. We knew that more often than not it would be Ann who would unpack his suitcase. And she did, so John had some quick thinking to do to explain how it got there.

One of the funniest things I witnessed was John munching away on some cake. Someone in the crew had baked the cake and they all knew, except John, what the ingredients were – the usual fruitcake mix but with an added ingredient, dope. The cake was brought out after one of the shows and left on the table for whoever wanted to have a slice. John dived in and had a slice and we held the laughter back as we saw him tuck into it. He must have liked it because he went back for a second and third slice.

Drugs weren't a major feature in The Jam's life. It was the seventies and eighties so of course there were drugs around. We used varying road crews too, so the type and choice of drugs varied. Mind you there always seemed to be plenty of enthusiasm when we heard a trip to Amsterdam was on the cards. Cocaine and marijuana were part of the industry really, accepted as being part of the deal. Thankfully, during The Jam's career there were never any major incidents or casualties. Drugs in our camp was more of a recreational pastime rather than habitual. The pressures on our road crew were often hard and they had to be on the ball. We were fortunate with our road crew – they were all grafters. By the time The Jam were in full swing I think we had all seen the effects that drugs had had on rock stars like Keith Moon and John Bonham and we had taken notice.

All of us in The Jam were fortunate in matters relating to health. Apart from the occasional scratch and bruise from a row, things were generally OK. However, I do remember the time when Paul suffered a bout of shingles or, to use the correct terminology, herpes zoster. It's a painful skin rash that often results in horrible blisters. I'm told that someone can be infected for years before it actually rears its ugly head, so god knows how and when Paul caught it. It must have been hell for Paul to live with, and all the time he had it we continued to do the shows. The doctor gave him some medication, which were some droplets that had to be put onto the affected areas. I was one of the people who did this for Paul on several occasions. Credit to Paul for not cancelling shows because it must have been painful for him to perform on stage and get all sweaty, but he never complained.

I almost got left behind in LA once at the end of a tour. The pressure was off, and I had an opportunity to relax. On the morning of our departure we had a few hours to kill so I arranged to meet up with some friends for lunch. I thought I would have plenty of time and I was having a nice lunch, a chat, a drink, but I didn't realise that my watch had stopped. I kept glancing at my watch and thinking, 'Is that all the time is, great, I've got ages left'. Then the reality hit as someone informed me what the real time was. I leaped up and raced back to the hotel, hoping to catch the others, but by the time I got back to the hotel everyone had checked out already, and my luggage and passport had gone with them. I ran outside and flagged down a cab. It was like a scene from a film as I instructed the driver to, 'Get me to the airport and step on it.' He didn't reply, but I was thrown back into the seat as we took off at speed. The pressure was on. I really didn't want to be responsible for delaying the flight or causing any upset amongst the band or crew, especially as this was right at the end of the tour and everyone just wanted to get home. Thankfully the cab driver got me there fast and I just managed to meet up with the others as they were checking in. There were a couple of frowns but it was OK.

In November The Jam went to Sweden to perform at a strange venue in a town called Lund. The venue was a large indoor funfair with loads of rides from merry-go-rounds to roller coasters and a fairly big stage to one side. The crew set about unloading the gear and all the rides were also being prepared for the night's activity. It was all very bizarre. As soon as we finished soundchecking we were invited to have a go on the rides, which we thought looked fairly tame and might be a laugh. We sat in these bubble shaped seats and got strapped in, and the ride began. We set off slowly with the ride going round and round. But then it started to pick up speed and elevation. I wasn't sure if I liked it but told myself that it would be all over in a couple of minutes. Only it didn't stop after a couple of minutes, the bastard controller kept the ride going for much longer. After about five minutes we were all feeling as sick as pigs and not enjoying it at all. It was like one of those endurance tests for astronauts.

Eventually it came to a stop but the controller was nowhere to be found. However, we were more concerned with trying to steady ourselves and stop from throwing up. It was soon after that we had to go and play the show. The sense of disorientation seemed to last for ages. That show was a struggle.

Festivals were often thrown into the regular gig list. In order to make sure I got to the airport in time for one festival, Dickie Bell, our tour manager, decided to stay at my flat the night before we were due to fly out to Europe. Dickie was a seasoned professional in the field who had worked for various rock bands before The Jam, so he had seen a few things in his time. The night before we were due to leave we cracked open a bottle of wine, one of the many bottles of Bull's Blood put aside from previous riders, then another and then another. We carried on drinking throughout the entire night and managed to polish off all but one bottle that I had saved, which we finished off in the cab on the way to the airport in the morning. I felt more pissed than I ever had before and, of course, we arrived late and missed our flight. All the other band members and crew had gone on ahead. All we could do was wait for the next available flight, which we did, in the airport bar. Fortunately, we weren't due to play that same day so we knew we had time to get to the festival and sober up before the show.

We finally got on the plane and of course ordered more drinks. By the time we landed, got a taxi to the festival and picked up our 'Access All Areas' passes, we were steaming. We made our way to the main stage and discovered The Kinks playing. But during our navigating to where we thought we needed to be we got a bit lost and ended up in the pit, the area between the stage and the audience. It had been raining so the pit area was wet and muddy, like being in the trenches. Dickie and I thought this was hilarious and started to fuck around, jumping over each other and so on, and every now and then we looked up to catch a glimpse of Ray Davies staring back at us. It was a bit surreal.

One of the festival crew spotted us and went to tell John and Kenny that we had arrived. They were not impressed when they saw us covered in mud and pissed out of our heads. We both got a bollocking for that.

I bumped into Joe Jackson at another festival. Backstage areas should be areas where only the band and those that needed to be there were allowed. Nowadays there seems to be two backstage areas, one where competition winners and liggers hang out, along with some press, and the other 'real' backstage area which was reserved just for the artists and that's where I would get to meet other bands, which was a more relaxed and rare opportunity.

Somehow a photographer had followed Joe Jackson into the backstage area and was really hassling him for a photograph. Jackson wasn't amused by this and kept telling the snapper to go away. But the photographer wasn't taking no for an answer and persisted, which I could see was winding Jackson up even further. It went on for a bit longer until Jackson properly lost it and told the snapper in no uncertain terms to fuck off and he meant it. Only then did the snapper understand and fade away into the shadows.

Although every effort was made for the shows to go without a hitch there were times when blunders were made. One of my most memorable was the time I got locked out of the Brighton Conference Centre. By the time The Jam was playing in venues as big as the Brighton Centre we had some money to pay for decent hotels. When we played in Brighton we stayed at the Grand, one of the Victorian seafront hotels on the Kings Road. There used to be passageways that led from the hotel directly into the Brighton Centre, and that's how we would get to the venue. We set off, escorted by Kenny, weaving our way through the various passageways but somehow I managed to lag behind. As I turned the last corner, I just caught sight of the fire doors being closed. I yelled out and ran but it was too late, Kenny closed the door and the others continued on their journey.

'Shit' I thought as I made my way back to the hotel. Once back there the only option I could think of was to walk round to the front doors of the Conference Centre. So I did that, thinking it would be straightforward. I set off but a small crowd spotted me and followed, hanging a few steps behind me. The crowd got bigger and by the time I reached the Conference Centre there was a fair size crowd surrounding me. I banged on the front doors, and kept banging until I eventually caught the attention of one of the security staff but he just kept mouthing back to me the words, 'We're not open yet.' I tried my best, through thick glass doors, to explain to him who I was and waving my 'All Areas Pass', but he wasn't having any of it. By now the crowd behind had swelled even more and now they were joining in, yelling at the guy inside, 'Let him in, he's in the band.' He still wasn't having any of it, more kids in the crowd joined in. 'Let him in you prat. He is the drummer in The Jam.' Then they started to bang and kick the door, but before it all got out of hand he finally figured out what was happening and let me inside... just in the nick of time.

I think it may have been Brighton again when Paul ran into some trouble with some fans. We had played the show and were being ushered out of the venue to the tour bus. At the time Paul was into wearing a long woolly scarf but as soon as fans saw him they rushed forward and grabbed hold of whatever they could. Somehow, someone to Paul's left managed to grab hold of the end of his scarf and as he was trying to get free the other end was being pulled by someone else. The scarf got pulled from two directions and as it did it gripped Paul's neck and got tighter and tighter. It became dangerous as Paul was being strangled. Kenny rushed in to try and sort it out just before Paul turned blue.

During The Jam years Bruce and I did have a few run-ins, but then we all did at various times. In July The Jam played some shows in Japan, Osaka, Kyoto and three in Tokyo. While there I bought a bottle of saké as a gift for someone and stuffed it into my hand luggage. However, for whatever reason Bruce decided he hadn't had enough to drink back in the airport bar, so without asking he helped himself to my bottle of saké while I was asleep. I wasn't impressed, plus it was useless as a gift half empty. We had words over that. Bruce and I had to be kept apart at Los Angeles airport for fear that we might continue the fight that had started on the plane. John and Kenny were well aware that US customs could be very twitchy and wouldn't tolerate us coming to blows on their doorstep, so they made Bruce stand in one queue and me in another. We needed to be kept as far away from each other as possible. Both Bruce and myself did manage to keep our cool long enough to get into the country but later that evening I went and knocked on his hotel door. He opened it and I punched him; then I walked away, satisfied that I had made my point.

Travelling the world and spending so much time together provided ample opportunities for both positive and negative moments. Thankfully, within The Jam it was more positive than negative. There's a silly detail I recall where we had all bought identical digital watches in Japan. What was great about those watches was that the display could be changed so that it showed a map of the world, and this had the added bonus of displaying what time zone the watch wearer was in. During a fight with Bruce his watch face got scratched to such an extent that the time couldn't be read. He was really gutted about that because he had a running joke that wherever we went, when someone asked him the time, he would reply, 'Where? In what country?' He thought this was very funny.

It wasn't just me and Bruce that would come to blows either. Paul had his moments and would just lash out. There are some photos of Bruce wearing dark glasses during a gig in Paris. That was because he had a shiner courtesy of Paul that he wanted to hide. But on the whole we got on pretty well and managed our own stresses.

Being in such intense situations wasn't just limited to 'band camp' either. There were incidents outside of the band dynamic too. It's been well documented – and I have read several different accounts – but I was in the Speakeasy Club the night Paul and Sid Vicious came to blows. Vic Smith had got Paul, Bruce and me membership to this exclusive club. The 'Speak' as it had been known by its members since the sixties was a small basement club at 48 Margaret Street near Oxford Circus. Opened in 1966, it became a popular retreat for music and media 'industry' types. Jimi Hendrix had been taken to the club soon after his arrival into the UK and The Who were also regulars. They even created a spoof jingle for the club – 'Speak easy, drink easy, pull easy' – amongst the other ads on their *Who Sell Out* album.

I went into the Speakeasy one evening with Alan Belcher. It wasn't that busy so we could easily see what 'faces' were also in the club. John Entwistle was sitting at one of the tables by himself. There were three empty seats beside him so we nudged each other and went to sit down. Within 20 minutes Alan and John were arm-wrestling. Now Alan, being a seasoned roadie was a fairly strong guy, but Entwistle was far superior and I could see for myself why he was nicknamed 'the Ox'. However much Alan pressed down on Entwistle's arm it wouldn't budge. The man really was as strong as an ox. He could see we were impressed and said, 'I've got muscles like these through playing bass with The Who.' We just grinned but didn't believe a word of it.

The night Paul and Vicious had a run-in was much busier. Some of the tables had benches rather than individual chairs and there was a lot of shoving and pushing. It was one of those nights that if you stood up to go the toilet or the bar, by the time you returned your seat was gone. There was a crowd of us and there was Vicious with some people and a girl who I presume was Nancy Spungen. Paul was sitting on the bench but Vicious also wanted to sit down and sort of pushed his way onto it, which Paul didn't like. I think Vicious must have said something to Paul too, because the next thing Paul had picked up a glass and whacked it around Sid's head. Tough nut Vicious didn't even respond, he simply exited the club.

That early punk era could be especially unnerving at times. In 1977 we played a gig in High Wycombe, The Nags Head, with a band called The Boys. They had been a punk band since the early days and had come out of another band called London SS. The Boys were our support act on that night and we had to share a dressing room with them. Things were a bit crowded and one of The Boys made some comment that caused a reaction in Paul. It all flared up and Paul reached for a light ale bottle and smashed it on a table. Threatening someone with a broken bottle is far more effective. Paul pointed the smashed bottle at his opponent but it didn't get the reaction he intended. Instead we all just stared at the bottle, well what was left of it. Paul had smashed virtually all of it away and only about an inch was left of the neck. It looked ridiculous and not exactly threatening. Having turned into a farce, it kind of negated the incident, and nothing more happened.

There was an especially troublesome night at the Embassy Cinema in Hove in April 1977. The venue was only a music venue for a short period and shut down soon after a Jam gig and then became the Black Cat bingo club until the late eighties. On the night of the Jam gig the crowd went for it, pulling seats up from the floor, smashing them up and hitting each other with bits of furniture. We watched the riot unfold before us from the stage, and very unnerving it was too, to the point where we had to stop playing and retreat into the backstage area for protection. A photographer in the house that night, Walt Davidson, was caught up in the action but he had his camera and film confiscated by the police so they could examine it and help them with their investigation into what had happened and who was involved. I think arrests were made because of the photos and the evidence used in court. This sort of thing happened less often as time went on, but in the early days, when the punk movement was still emerging from London, spitting and violence made headlines in the British press and was copied by others as the thing to do at 'punk shows'. It was the press – who exaggerated it and created misconceptions – that caused the problems as much as the punks.

At another gig we were playing in Scandinavia, the local motorbike boys heard there was a 'punk gig' and all that went with it, in their town. So they rode up, burst in and proceeded to pick a fight with the punters. Once again we left the stage a bit quick.

CHAPTER TEN

The Vapors appeared onto our radar after Bruce has seen them play in Guildford. Suitably impressed with what he heard, he got John involved with them on the managerial side. Through John The Vapors got a record contract and some studio time was arranged and Vic Smith was pulled in to produce their first album, *New Clear Days*, a really good collection of great pop songs.

Off the back of The Vapors' relationship with John they got support slots with The Jam. We all got on well and the fun began. Prank followed prank. They had a crew member who we would constantly wind up. We would say things like, 'In the morning can you go down to the shops to buy everybody a copy of the *Melody Maker*, *Sounds* and *NME*?' We thought he would come back with just a few copies of each mag; instead he returned with a huge pile, one for each member of both bands and their crew and management. He must have cleared the newsagents out. The thing was we only wanted to read some little article that we had heard might be in the current issue. So we grabbed him and gaffer-taped him to a chair and left him in the hotel car park. We left him there for ages until somebody took pity and freed him.

The Vapors would do stuff to us and we would return the favour.

One time while they were on stage we entered their dressing room, gathered up all their clothes and stuck them to the ceiling. We had help from our crew that day and it was a well-executed plan of gatherers, stickers and lookouts. On coming off stage The Vapors found our prank to be most amusing... not!

The Vapors reached number three in the charts and number 36 in the States with their song 'Turning Japanese'. Many at the time thought the song was about masturbation, but their frontman Dave Fenton has since denied this. The band did well out of that track because at the time there was a strike in the American TV industry and as a result loads of programmes got pulled and replaced with old programmes and these included re-runs of *Godzilla*. Those *Godzilla* programmes and films had been made in Japan and somehow The Vapors' song got connected to this and it reached countless Americans who had some 'in-joke' that they were turning Japanese. The year 1980 was very good for them but they split up in 1982 – there must have been something in the air that year!

The Jam were kept busy and we went off to play in Sweden and again, having time to kill and being in need of food, we went to find a restaurant. The hotel we were staying in overlooked this large square that had various bars, shops and restaurants contained within it. We sat down and ordered our food and waited and waited for it to arrive; and when it did, it wasn't that great. Then we ordered more drinks which took ages to be served too. The whole service was very poor and when we decided we had had enough we tried to get the waiter's attention so we could settle the bill. We tried our best but got no response. So we got up and casually walked out. However, once we got out into the square someone suggested it may be better if we legged it, so we did and all ran back to the hotel. We got away with that one.

Joe Awome got into some trouble on that trip. One of the three 'personal security' guys assigned to The Jam, he was an aspiring boxer who'd had the privilege of going two rounds with Muhammad Ali in an exhibition fight. Kenny Wheeler looked after Paul, often regarded as 'the gooseberry duty'. I was mostly with Chris Adoja and Joe was with Bruce although he sometimes dreaded it.

Joe was arrested in Sweden after some misunderstanding and wrongful finger pointing. One of the locals who was hanging about the venue before the show had run into some trouble and been beaten up. He went to the police and told them that a big black guy in The Jam entourage was the offender. I think this fan had been causing trouble and making a nuisance of himself most of the afternoon. He wanted to get into the soundcheck because he had no ticket for the show.

What I heard was that some other fans took it on themselves to 'sort' this guy out and did just that, a pretty good job too. For reasons known only to him he pointed the finger at Joe rather than the real offenders and the police came to arrest Joe. We knew it was a mistake. We knew Joe well, from way back, when he worked at Michael's Club as a bouncer in Woking, when he would stand at the top of the stairs, only letting those in who had a tie. So the claim that Joe would have done this was out of character, it just wasn't the sort of thing that he would have done. Joe was carted off to the police station and I think John went to sort things out. The truth did eventually come out and Joe was released without charge.

Joe has passed away now sadly, but I went to see him about three months before he died and he told me then he was due to go into hospital to have a brain tumour removed. He'd had it for years and it was regarded as benign but he'd decided to have it removed, even though he knew there were risks. Joe died on the operating table and it was a great loss because he was a lovely guy.

In 1980 I actually found myself getting a mortgage and putting down a deposit on a house. I had moved out from Croydon and found a place, a two-up, two-down, that I liked and could afford in Lightwater, which is just outside Woking. The deposit was £2,000, a huge amount of money back then. The house itself was a whacking £23,000 and needed lots of work. I had fronted one of the fireplaces with old stock bricks, which took me weeks to finish. I had not done a great job but it did look rustic. John Weller did the other fireplace in a day and made a much better job.

That year was shaping up to be very busy, what with touring, moving into my own house and going to the studio to record our fifth album, *Sound Affects*. The album was released in November and would become our highest charting album to date, reaching number two.

With each album that we recorded we consciously tried to take a new approach and I think each album demonstrates this. Resting on our laurels was never an option for us as a band or Paul as a songwriter. Pushing boundaries was the order of the day and when we went into Townhouse Studios to record *Sound Affects*, this was our intention. We now had much more studio experience and we had settled down with Vic Smith and his way of doing things.

Vic had his method of working and this helped to turn *Sound Affects* into what it became. The production side of the album was all important and I think that contributed to why Vic wasn't used for *The Gift*. I think we wanted to return to a more basic way of doing things for that album.

During the recording of *Sound Affects* we included all sorts of ideas from percussion and sound effects and even someone speaking in French. To this day I have no idea what that French person is saying. I think it was a contact of Paul's and he got him into the studio. I don't remember being present at the time of the recording though. For one track we even tried to record a plastic cup being trodden on. Another experiment was to try and capture the sound of a bottle breaking. To achieve this we got a couple of wine bottles and wrapped them in plastic bags – to reduce the inevitable mess – while I tried to smash them in time with the music. We spent a long time trying to get the timing right but even longer clearing up the tiny pieces of broken glass.

Townhouse was a really good studio to work in and easy for us all to get to. I stayed in one of the band flats above the studio while we recorded the album. Some of the inner sleeve photos were taken in Townhouse. This was around the time that I was trying to sport a beard but it didn't last long and I have never tried since.

It was while we were recording *Sound Affects* that Phil Collins broke my tambourine. In between recording most of us would hang about in a room near the reception where there was a TV with chairs and a sofa. I would sometimes see Phil's girlfriend there and we would relax, chat and go round to the off-licence, buy wine and get slaughtered together.

At the time Collins was recording his *Face Value* album, from which his hit 'In The Air Tonight' was lifted. He used the studio during the night and The Jam used the studio during the day. One morning after I had stayed in the upstairs flat I ambled down to the reception area and spotted my broken tambourine. I walked over to where it was on the table and sat beside the tambourine was a bottle of champagne, a bottle of orange juice and a note from Phil Collins apologising for breaking it.

There was another Genesis connection while we recorded at Townhouse. During one of the sessions Peter Gabriel popped in to say hello. I felt quite in awe and honoured to meet him and set about telling him about my interpretation of 'Solsbury Hill'. He listened to what I had to say then calmly replied, 'Nah, it's nothing to do with that' and then he left. That was the extent of our conversation.

Reflecting back on The Jam years the recording part was only fleeting moments really. For me the birth of a song, then the rehearsing and recording gets skipped over quite quickly. Most of my memories of the songs are of playing them live. That's what we did most of all.

I had a long drive to do recently and decided to put a CD of *Sound Affects* on the car stereo. It was good to do and I enjoyed listening to it; it also brought back some memories of those recording sessions. It had been years since I last heard the album and afterwards it felt nice. It's much nicer playing Jam songs now after all those years.

Thinking back on that period between 1980 and 1982 it was pretty relentless. We were literally being swept along by the momentum of the success that we were having. And the more success we achieved the more demanding everything became. All we could do was allow ourselves to go with the flow. Much of that period is simply a blur. But we were doing exactly what we wanted to do and it was great.

The single lifted from *Sound Affects* was 'Start', which went to number one in September, our second number one of the year after 'Going Underground' which had hit the top spot in February. The news of its position reached us while we were on tour in America. It was thought it would chart high because we knew our fanbase had swollen in the last year. 'Going Underground' hadn't crept up the charts either; it had rocketed into the number one slot taking everyone by surprise. The demand for it was massive and Polydor sensed this. Having The Jam get a number one single delighted Polydor and rightly so.

Even though getting a number one record had never been our absolute goal it still felt fabulous. I think Paul and Bruce shared in my elation. It was a great achievement, and everyone told us so. We made our excuses and bailed out of the American tour and returned to England. We were number one in England and needed to be there to enjoy it. Concorde was booked (which wasn't cheap) and we flew home... quickly.

Having a number one didn't seem to change things that much really. Certainly as individuals nothing changed. We had been on the rise since 1977, so getting a number one was just like passing through one set of clouds at a certain height but being able to see the next lot in the way. The next lot of clouds turned out to be 'Start'.

It was great being part of something that wasn't driven by the desire or need to have a chart position. It was great that we could release a song like 'Going Underground' as a stand-alone record. It wasn't lifted from an album but if it had it would have helped to sell more albums. But we didn't only release singles that were included on albums and this was a very deliberate thing to do on our part.

Of course, having two number one records in the same year attracted a certain amount of both media and public attention and accolades. While with The Jam we were privileged to be awarded several gold discs, which are handed out on record sales, not positions in the charts. I got a gold disc for 'In The City' in 1983 as it had taken that long for it to sell the required amount to warrant a gold disc status. I heard in the nineties that some Jam albums reached platinum disc status, but I was never handed one. I don't think Paul or Bruce were either.

Following the success of 'Start' we continued with our planned tour and spent pretty much the remainder of the year on the road; our last gig of the year on December 14 in the Coliseum at St Austell in Cornwall. Then we had a break and our annual Christmas party. Having number one records also gave us a certain amount of power that we hadn't had before, and we found that we had a bit more say in our own careers. There was definitely a turning point for The Jam that year. We even shared the front cover of *Smash Hits* with Madness and Peter Gabriel! It was indicative of how things changed. We went from spending years chasing the press but after two number one records they chased us. It was a nice position to be in, and we were able to pick and choose what we wanted to do.

We had a decent breather after Christmas and didn't play any shows until February, and when we did it was on our terms and what we chose to do was unusual. I'm not sure whose idea it was, but we all thought it would be good to play a few local venues and give something back. On February 14 we played at the Cricketers, a local pub in Westfield, Woking, and then on the 16th we played in the Woking YMCA. They even gave us honorary membership cards for a year. However, I nearly ran over a guy in the car park across the road. I hadn't noticed him when I got into the car (I had a TR6 at the time). It was only when I started the engine that I saw his head pop up from under the bonnet. It turned out that he was trying to unscrew my number plate and nick it. He didn't have time to finish the job but ran off instead.

Then, on February 17, we played in Sheerwater Youth Club. It was a very unfussy set of gigs with basic small stages and minimal gear. We played short sets to very enthusiastic audiences. Nevertheless some of the locals in the Cricketers didn't especially like what we were doing; that their pub had been overrun with parka-clad mods who had turned up on their scooters that had filled up the car park. Tensions rose and after a complaint from Pat, Bruce's girlfriend at the time, Kenny had to drag one of the locals out into the car park where he gave him a 'knuckle sandwich'. Such was the sandwich that Kenny returned to the pub with a tooth stuck into his fist. Apparently the recipient of Kenny's attentions had upset Pat, and Bruce told Kenny who dealt with it.

We played shows in virtually every month throughout 1981, returning to Japan and Canada again. We didn't release any albums but did release three singles, 'That's Entertainment', 'Funeral Pyre' and 'Absolute Beginners'. Both 'Funeral Pyre' and 'Absolute Beginners' got into the Top 10 while 'That's Entertainment' was actually a German import but it still sold well.

Around the time of 'Absolute Beginners' we did a photo shoot in Chiswick Park off the A4 in west London. Paul liked the location, assuming that the natural background would lend itself to attractive pictures; also The Beatles had done a photo shoot there in 1966, making promotional films for 'Paperback Writer' and its B-side 'Rain'. On the day the camera duties fell to a young amateur photographer named Derek D'Souza, a fan of The Jam who had sent Ann some pics that he had taken of us on stage. I think he used to sneak his camera into gigs, but Ann had shown Paul and John and they had liked what they saw and Derek was invited to take the photographs in Chiswick Park. Derek had sat in on some studio time in Air while we had been recording 'Tales From The Riverbank'.

I still see Derek around and he recently took some photos of The Brompton Mix, a band I manage. He told me about how he and a bunch of other Jam fans managed to get into a gig via an unauthorised entrance, like a scene from *The Great Escape* only in reverse because from where they were hiding they could only rush into the crowd when one of the spotlights swung past them. They had to take turns and time it just right so they didn't get spotted. Unfortunately Derek got caught and got slung out.

We did lots of photo sessions but the Chiswick Park shoot was memorable because we'd already established that the photos would be used for the 'Absolute Beginners' single sleeve and one of Derek's pics was used on the back cover. I suspect Derek felt nervous but we didn't give him any trouble. We were quite good at taking instructions so when Derek asked us to stand by a certain object doing a certain thing we complied. We were never into the modelling side of things so most of The Jam's photos show us just being ourselves sitting or standing around doing nothing much, just looking natural.

Some of the photos saw us standing next to big statues and on large stone steps and peering through austere black gates. Photoshoots in outside locations always offered up something unique. When we did the shoot for the pics that ended up in the inner sleeve for *Sound Affects* we had to get up really early to catch the mist as it drifted across a lake.

The combination of the location and Derek's eye did produce a collection of pictures that captured a special atmosphere. It was an August day and warm. I wore a red and white pin-stripe shirt and a blazer which I still have, and I'm wearing a pair of boxing boots too – Joe Awome's influence. My sponsorship deal with Lonsdale came around because of Joe, and I remember visiting Lonsdale's flagship store in London and leaving with several pairs of boxing boots. I found them ideal for playing drums because they were lightweight and had grip. The only downside was that it took a month of Sundays to lace them up. I also had a sweatshirt made up that instead of saying 'Lonsdale London' on the chest had 'Buckler Woking' in the same logo.

We shot the video for 'Absolute Beginners' in the terraced streets around Nomis studios, in the area of Shepherd's Bush behind

Olympia. The cameraman had Paul, Bruce and me chasing the rear of the car with the camera aimed at us. You can see from the video that none of us particularly enjoy running. Going to a gym or doing exercise wasn't a favoured pastime in the Jam camp. The only occasion when I gave running a go was with Joe Awome who was well into his fitness for boxing and would get up early in the morning to go for a run. He managed to convince me that it was a good idea too so I agreed to go with him one morning when we were staying at a hotel in Berlin. Someone loaned me a tracksuit and I met Joe in the hotel lobby, all fired up, punching the air and ready to do it. We left the hotel, turned the corner and were hit by a freezing cold wind which almost cut me in half. Joe wasn't going to be stopped, though, and sped off. I followed for a few hundred yards but gave up and ambled back to the hotel. And that was the extent of my keep fit campaign.

Shooting the 'Funeral Pyre' video was an entirely different experience. We went to Horsell Common, just outside of Woking, and used the old sandpit that HG Wells had incorporated into his book *The War Of The Worlds*. Wells had discovered the area during the mid-1800s when he lived in Woking.

Someone thought it would be a suitable location for 'Funeral Pyre' and we trotted off down there. It was decided that a giant bonfire should be built, and to help build it we invited a number of our local friends and family to help out. They can be seen carrying the lumps of wood in the video. The Carver brothers were involved, and Paul's sister Nicky too. It was an impressive blaze. I had to move my drum kit several times because the skins kept getting damaged from bits flying off the fire, and afterwards I had to send it back to Premier to have the drums recovered.

When I was in the band Time UK, after The Jam split up, I suggested Horsell Common as a setting for some photos of that band too. While we were taking the pics an elderly gentleman appeared who lived in a cottage on the common. He ambled over to us and asked what we were doing. We explained that we were a band to which he replied, 'Ah you're a band are you? Well I hope you don't set fire to the place like some bloody band did a few years ago!' I just shuffled away and kept quiet.

'Funeral Pyre' was a great song to play. It opened with my snare drum beat, then Bruce joined in and Paul followed. We ended up recording it three times in more than one studio because we weren't satisfied with the initial attempts. I don't recall what the problem was but I remember that we had to work hard on the song to get it how we wanted it to sound, and funnily enough that turned out to be the first version we recorded. This sort of thing did happen occasionally.

I don't know how I found the time but in 1981 I was asked to drum on some demos for Stuart Adamson. Previous to Big Country Stuart had played in The Skids who had had a hit in 1979 with 'Into The Valley'. He was trying to get his new band Big Country off the ground and the demos were used to help get a record deal. I still have an old cassette tape of those songs. Eventually Adamson recruited Mark Brzezicki, Tony Butler and along with Bruce Watson, Big Country was formed. They went on to release some great songs like 'Fields Of Fire' and 'In A Big Country', and they supported The Jam.

We also went into Air Studios to record new songs that would find their way onto *The Gift* album. We hadn't used Air before and changing studios was a way of avoiding getting stuck into a fixed routine of doing things. Air was owned by Beatles producer George Martin, and the first time I walked into Air I was in awe of this brand new studio that had a small suite with the first digital recording equipment I'd ever seen. It looked impressive but we didn't understand any of it. One day while we were working in the studio the door opened and we heard a familiar scouse accent. We all swung around in unison to face Paul McCartney. He was friendly enough, greeted us and explained that he was doing some mixing of his own songs in the room next door. And then he was gone. That was, so far, the only time I have ever met a Beatle.

It was a brief encounter with McCartney but looking back the years have been filled with numerous brief encounters; people are often too busy, or being ushered into a tour bus or into an interview. I remember playing a gig in the States and as I glanced to the side of the stage I saw Mick Jagger, his arms crossed, seemingly enjoying what he heard. Unfortunately, by the time we finished our set and got off stage he'd vanished so we never actually got to meet him. Steve Gibbons showed up at another gig; again I noticed him standing in the wings and again he'd also vanished by the time we got off stage.

Air Studios was in a prime location, on the top floor of a building just off Oxford Street, and it was on the roof that the photos for *The Gift* album cover were shot by the photographer Twink. It seemed as convenient a place as any to do a photo shoot, and because we knew we were doing the shoot, we each brought what clothes we wanted to wear. Twink then took photos of us literally running on the spot, but after he showed us what he'd done Bruce decided he didn't like the trousers he was wearing and wanted to do his photo shoot again. Twink was called back to Air and he and Bruce went back up onto the roof. It seemed a bit unnecessary really, especially because we already knew that the photos were going to be treated to give them that red, green and amber look; and Bruce's trousers would pretty much look just like any old trousers in the end.

We finished recording *The Gift* which was released in March of 1982, a few weeks after our third number one single, 'A Town Called Malice'. We lifted the song from the album and included 'Precious' as the B-side. This was the only track from the album that I didn't like and I still don't. It just didn't seem to work and didn't seem to be a Jam song, if there is such a thing as a Jam song. Paul had presented the song to us and explained that he wanted to do something with a hint of a disco overtone. When it came out I heard it said that it sounded more like a rip off of Pigbag. One night I went to a disco and took a cassette tape of the song and gave it to the DJ and asked him to play it. He did and it cleared the dance floor. Nevertheless, considering all the songs that we did, it's a pretty good track record for me to only dislike one.

In the bigger picture 'Precious' didn't take anything away from *The Gift* which became our first number one album. We had done it. We now had number one singles and a number one album. Most of April and May was spent on tour promoting *The Gift* and then we had a break in the summer. It was on Paul's return from his holiday in Italy that he told us he was leaving The Jam.

The summer was tinged by more sad news. In August our old friend and early Jam member Dave Waller died from a heroin overdose. He was found in one of the accommodation rooms above the Wheatsheaf pub in Woking. There were a lot of heightened emotions running around. The Falklands War dominated the news and had a huge impact on my generation. I was actually on holiday in Gibraltar when the British fleet returned and I could see the bullet and shell marks on the sides of the battleships.

To finish off the year, The Jam went back on tour and we released two more singles, 'The Bitterest Pill' and 'Beat Surrender'. 'Just Who Is The Five O' Clock Hero' had been made available, albeit as another import like 'That's Entertainment'. Keith Thomas and Steve Nichol had joined us in the studio around the time of recording *The Gift*, as the songs suited a brass section. At that time we had enough money in the band kitty to afford to take them on the road with us too. They were fabulous musicians, as can be heard on a track like 'Circus' where they really lock in with the drums. Their brass parts were simple but effective and really enhanced the songs on *The Gift*.

The brass section was taken on the Trans Global tour and it was a really great tour. We seemed to put something extra into it. There may have been an element of us trying to say to Paul, 'Look we are really good and we're proving that we are really good, so what the fuck do you think you're doing?' Bruce and I could have taken the view of bollocks to it all and just gone through the motions but we didn't and instead we really went for it.

'Beat Surrender', The Jam's final single, went to number one in November. Tracie Young, another contact that came about via Paul, sang backing vocals on the song, joining us in Air Studios to record her parts. She was very young, only about 17, and she also joined us on *Top Of The Pops* when we performed the song. It must have been quite an experience for her, not just to sing on a Jam song but to actually sing on The Jam's final song. Paul was in the early stages of setting up his Respond Records project, and he signed The Questions and Tracie who went on to enjoy some success while on the label. The music was very much of the time. Paul's girlfriend, Gill Price, was photographed waving a white flag and that was used for the front cover. I don't quite know what the thinking was behind that. Maybe it did indicate a surrendering of something, but as ever with Paul there could be many interpretations. Contained on the inside cover of the single was a picture of the band by a spiral staircase, the fire escape. That picture was taken at Stanhope Place, the studio owned by Polydor that was where Solid Bond Studios was eventually located. In December *Dig The New Breed* was released and that was that until the compilation album *Snap* appeared in late 1983. The Jam was finished.

CHAPTER ELEVEN

Coming out of Christmas 1982 and heading into the New Year, I felt I had nothing to look forward to. It wasn't so much depressing as frustrating. For years I always had some idea of what lay ahead, a bit like driving a car and keeping an eye on the traffic in front of you. Once the Christmas celebrations had come and gone it really started to dawn on me that I needed to do something. I wanted to get a new band together and I wanted to get back out on the road, so I began to steer my efforts towards that. I knew what I needed to do first was to find a songwriter, so I put out feelers to see who might be around, willing and available.

A few weeks into the New Year through various referrals and contacts I was put in touch with a guy called Ray Simone. A meeting was arranged and he came to my home. We hit it off right from the start and I found him to be a refreshing character after the angst and stress that I had been around in those last months of The Jam. However, Ray wasn't a prolific songwriter and he suggested I meet an old band member of his named Jimmy Edwards. They had both been in a five-piece band called Masterswitch that was signed to Epic Records, part of CBS, in 1978 and released one song called 'Action Replay' before splitting up the following year.

Their efforts had been pretty much overshadowed by all the media and attention that their punk peers and labelmates The Clash were getting.

I had heard of Jimmy and his Masterswitch, but I didn't know much about him apart from that he had been signed to Polydor and had released his own version of 'In The City' in 1981. He had also done some work with Sham 69, helping to put the finishing touches to some of their songs.

The band Time UK formed with me on drums, Ray on guitar and Jimmy on vocals. We breathed some new life into some songs from the Masterswitch catalogue but we felt the band was incomplete and so arranged auditions for a bassist and lead guitar. The first bass player was Martin Gordon from Radio Stars and Sparks but we only did one show with him, a warm-up show at the Kings of Wessex School, the gig secured by my brother John who was teaching there at the time. We seemed to go down quite well despite the fact that Martin went on stage dressed as an operatic clown. We were as surprised as the pupils. He was a very good bass player but he didn't really fit in. Jimmy was all for sacking him but didn't have the courage to do so and so the unenviable task fell to me at the next rehearsal. Credit to Martin, he took it in his stride and graciously bowed out. More auditions were arranged and this was when Nick South entered the picture.

Nick had plenty of previous experience and had worked with Sniff'n'The Tears, the Steve Marriott All-Stars and Yoko Ono while his first ever gig was playing with bluesman Alexis Korner. He played an Alembic bass, an expensive instrument and his pride and joy and he was, without doubt, a very talented bass player. Of all the bass players I had seen in my studio or on the road or have worked with, he was the most versatile. We clicked together, which is an important aspect for any rhythm section. We still needed another guitarist so next up to join the band was Danny Kustow, formerly of the Tom Robinson Band. He was so nervous at the audition that he turned up with a bottle of brandy concealed in a brown paper bag, and every now and again we could spot him taking swigs from it.

He would say to us 'was that all right' to which we would answer yes. Then he would then take another swig. He was just one of those guys with a nervous disposition but we were all a bit nervous really because we were all new to each other. We did, however, like his maverick personality and we took to him immediately.

The Time UK line-up became Nick South on bass, me on drums, Jimmy Edwards on vocals and Danny Kustow (later replaced by Fletcher Christian) and Ray Simone on guitars. It was exciting but there was plenty of apprehension. I had been in The Jam for years and my life had been relatively stable but now I found myself in a band where no one knew what was going to happen next.

Initially we rehearsed in a studio in Copperfield Street in London, located under some train arches. Some rooms next door were occupied by Vince Clarke of Yazoo and this meant that there were always these new electronic wave musicians hanging about. It was the time of the New Romantics so there was a lot of big hair, big shoulder pads and frilly shirts. It was evident to everyone that the whole new wave/punk era was coming to an end. The Pistols were long gone, Billy Idol had broken away and headed for America and Joe Strummer had fired Mick Jones from The Clash.

Then there was MTV pushing its way in, which meant bands simply had to produce videos to promote their songs. The video really did kill the radio star. Some of this came the way of The Jam but we were incredibly uncomfortable with it; it just wasn't in us to do that sort of thing. Polydor insisted, of course, and we had to have a video for the singles but if you look at those Jam videos they are quite desperate affairs, certainly nowhere near as slick as the sort of videos that bands like Duran Duran were making. We didn't get the shoots that included lounging about on yachts and sitting beside swimming pools surrounded by beautiful woman. What we got was the Carvers painting backdrops and running up the street.

There wasn't much about that eighties period that I liked. The Pete Shelley solo album was OK. That was an unexpected project from someone like Pete in that it was all machine based, quite polished but very different from anything that he did with

Buzzcocks. The way songs were being produced on record was also changing. Overproduced in many ways, Bowie's *Let's Dance* was around too and although I liked the songs the production had a very plastic sound. Time UK was still very much based in that rawer, punk rock, new wave sound and there wasn't much demand for that from the industry.

I still loved that live band mentality; it's what I had been a part of and known for over a decade. Also, The Jam had only been over a matter of months before, so the group, along with Paul and Bruce, were far from a distant memory for me. On two or three occasions I dropped into the studios that Paul had bought from Polydor and renamed Solid Bond. They were located in a lovely protected building just north of Hyde Park and Polydor sold out because the lease was up and they decided that they didn't need them any more. This was another sign of the times; record companies once had recording studios all over London but they were beginning to disappear. With studios closing Paul and John Weller saw an opportunity, assuming they could pay for their own recordings; by owning the studio they could in effect give themselves the bill. So I dropped into Solid Bond a few times, knowing that Paul would be there, simply to say hello but he would never come out to see me. After this happened a few times I just gave up and I've only ever seen Paul on one occasion since.

One night I went to see Bruce's band play and I spotted Paul, who was just on his way out. I leaned forward to say hello and he replied with a brief hello back and just continued to walk on. That was that, the last time Paul and I actually spoke to each other, and as long ago as 1983.

I did stay in touch with Bruce who had released a solo single called 'Freak'. Me, my wife, Lesley, Bruce and his wife, Pat, would occasionally meet up and go for a meal and a drink. I discovered that Bruce was also finding it hard to stay in contact with Paul. It was as if Paul just didn't want to know us any longer. Paul wouldn't even talk to the press about The Jam either; he just wanted to talk about The Style Council and what he was doing there and then, which I could understand. But it was as if he was completely dismissing what The Jam had been for him and what we had achieved. And both Bruce and I felt like we were being dismissed too. It felt very unfair; after all, all we wanted to do was stay in touch with each other really.

I remember Chris Parry telling me about an occasion when Bruce was in the Polydor office and he'd called Paul up. Chris got through and explained that Bruce was in the office with him and wouldn't mind a chat, for old time's sake, but Paul refused and wouldn't even stay on the line. Chris just couldn't understand it. It wasn't even as if the three of us had even fallen out over anything.

There is something in Paul's nature which leads him to behave that way. Another example was his relationship with Steve Brookes. When Steve left The Jam, Paul simply cut him out of his life until many years later. They are friends again nowadays and recently Paul even joined Steve on stage at another Wake Up Woking fund-raiser. It's something that Paul does; he did the same with his girlfriend Gill and a few others. Once someone falls out of Paul's circle they are 100% out of that circle.

After The Jam neither Bruce nor myself though Paul's behaviour would apply to us. But it did and I didn't understand it for a very long time. I continued to send Christmas cards but eventually stopped that as he never sent one back. It was such a shame; for years Paul, Bruce and me had been in a bubble together. It was like a fairy story: we had gone to school together, grown up together, spent years running around working men's clubs, we spent all our weekends together, drank together, we had number one records together, toured all over the world, we meant something to a lot of people, so what could possibly have gone wrong? In many ways the fairy tale had a sad ending. It was so hard to understand why Bruce and myself got the cold shoulder, but we did and this is how it has remained. I know that Bruce has been back in touch with Paul in recent years, so that is at least something.

Back in 1983, for months, Time UK worked towards getting a collection of songs together, surrounding ourselves with what we thought were the right people and getting ourselves into the position where we could go on the road. What we then discovered was that the whole musical scene had changed dramatically. All of a sudden it seemed as if every band was more electronic and keyboard led. Lots of bands had discarded the acoustic drummer and had opted for electronic drum machines. The 'real' band thing simply wasn't the flavour of the month any more. This meant that Time UK wasn't tailor-made for the mainstream. Nevertheless, we did manage to get a deal and have a single released. We managed to repeat this three more times but just couldn't get a label to commit to doing an album for us. Even Ray Simone's older brother, who was the managing director of Arista, couldn't sign us because it would look inappropriate.

Resigned to the lack of record label support, we took the songs on the road anyway. I think our early gigs were probably our best. We played at universities and some of the established rock clubs such as the Marquee in Wardour Street.

I took the lead in trying to get Time UK a deal. I used contacts I had made from The Jam days. I even took our demos to Polydor but they didn't seem that interested. In the end Red Bus Records released our debut single, 'The Cabaret', backed with 'Remember Days'. We recorded these songs in three different studios, The Music Works, Good Earth and Red Bus, simply because they were available when we needed them for recording and mixing down. It was produced by Robbie Farnon and he did a great job getting the hard hitting sound that we all liked and felt confident with.

Unfortunately Danny Kustow left soon after the release of 'The Cabaret' due to personal problems. He was missed as we had always counted on him to pull out the stops. He never failed to surprise and his live performances added a great deal to our sound. Plus there was the funny, if not odd, things that he would do, like the time he showed up at a Christmas party in a lovely old Georgian flat in Kensington, dressed in a tweed skirt, long black wig and angora sweater; this quite freaked out my wife, Lesley.

Lesley had seen some things over the years. We had known one another since 1978 and were married in August 1985. I met her in a pub called the Robin Hood in Woking and we got chatting and it went from there.

Lesley had been there for me since the very early days of The Jam's recording career, and I tried to be there for her when I had to. I remember that when we were recording *The Gift* album, I had a call informing me that the freezing weather had burst a pipe in the loft. I went back into the studio and told Paul what was happening and that I needed to go home and sort things out. It was about seven at night, and for some reason Paul got the right hump with this. But it was more important for me to go home and sort out the pipe; poor Lesley didn't know what to do or who to call.

Bruce and his wife, Pat, got together around 1979 or '80. Before that, in the mid-seventies when he was doing his apprenticeship with Unwin Brothers, a local printers, he was engaged to a girl named Joy. It was only when The Jam got closer to getting a record deal that Bruce rethought the situation and decided that he didn't want to get married. But then he met Pat and she was there for him throughout his Jam years.

Both Lesley and Pat got on very well and Pat was lovely, a really nice person. We spent a lot of time as a foursome doing things together when we had the girls on the road with us. Both Lesley and Pat travelled to places like Japan with us and there were times when we flew over to Jersey for short breaks, not only with our wives but with our parents too, all staying in the same hotel. We really enjoyed doing that as we all got on quite well and it was a real treat for my mum and dad. Paul didn't really get involved with things like those trips; he tended to isolate himself more. When he was with Gill they would often go off together and do their own thing. Some days you just couldn't get daylight between them.

Thankfully, both Lesley and Pat were there for Bruce and me when The Jam split up. For their part they simply carried on; I mean Lesley always worked anyway. She's always had a day job and maintained her own independence in that way. When the band split up we were still doing loads of work on our home in Lightwater. We had been building something together for many years by this point, and so we just carried on. Being away a lot during those years meant I had lost contact with a lot of my old school friends, and I suppose to varying degrees we had all gone our own way in the world. Lesley had stayed in touch with most of her friends from Winston Churchill School, and these old friends are still of great value to us.

Once The Jam had finished there was no desire or reason to do anything too dramatic, like move away from the area. Looking back now, those days straight after The Jam were filled with uncertainty. For a time I had no direction and found it hard to see where things were going. I woke up one day and found that I was effectively unemployed, presented with an emptiness that I wasn't familiar with and I had to find ways to fill that void. Lesley was there for me, a great support, in the same way that Pat was there for Bruce.

If anything I think Bruce was more devastated than me over the band splitting up. For years everything that we did rotated around The Jam. Paul, Bruce and myself needed each other, and the band wouldn't have achieved what it did without the three of us having the same goal. We had all helped each other so much, so naturally, that I suspect we just didn't realise it at the time. But, like me, Bruce did the right thing and got to work again, playing music with a new bunch of musicians. In time Lesley and I did move away from Lightwater to Sunningdale, a village not too far away. We remained in Sunningdale for about six years and lived there whilst Time UK was happening.

In the beginning we wanted to call ourselves just Time, but discovered there was already a band called that and we were at risk of running into problems over this. Because they were American we simply decided to add UK to Time to give us Time UK. It was an unusual name for the period; even using UK wasn't that popular. People tended to use Britain or England rather than UK.

After Danny Kustow left we held a series of auditions and Fletcher Christian was chosen to replace him. Completely unknown, he was very competent and full of enthusiasm. We carried on gigging but it took us a year to negotiate a new record deal even though 'The Cabaret' had sold very well. The problem we faced was a lack of organisation and co-ordination. Only after the record was released did someone realise that promotion was necessary for it to succeed. Timing is all important in the rock world and it seemed to work properly for Time UK. I had been used to the well-oiled machine and industry professionals that surrounded The Jam, Martin Hopewell from the Cowbell agency, and Dennis Munday and Chris Parry from Polydor. With The Jam there was planning, our activities set out and organised several months in advance. But with Time UK we just seemed to go from one small event to another small event. Things felt disconnected.

We soon parted company with our first manager, Terry McLellen, who had secured us the deal with Red Bus. Terry probably did his best but he struggled to find a way forward for us. He didn't know where best to place us, and not having any proper backing from the record label didn't help him either. Thankfully Radio One DJ Mike Read put us in contact with a guy called Michael Cohen and in November 1984 he took over as the band's manager. I think Mike Read may have even been managed by Michael too. I had known Mike from The Jam when he'd been very supportive, and he once presented a cheque to a charity at one of our shows at the Guildford Civic. He was one of the best DJs from that era.

Michael had been managing Schnorbitz, a St Bernard dog, among other TV personalities. He was an astute guy with offices in Hammer House, the old home of the Hammer horror films, in Soho's Wardour Street. Like McLellen, Michael also found us hard to place. His background was rooted in TV personalities, not bands, and especially not bands like Time UK. However, he had a wealth of connections and we thought he was our best shot at that time.

Michael was forever calling meetings at his office, so we would all trudge down there and there would always be a massive spread of lavish sandwiches laid on. This became a running joke, Jimmy especially liked this and on the journeys to the meetings with me he would always be trying to guess what flavour sandwich would be presented.

We would sit through these meetings, scoffing the sandwiches and listening to Michael's proposals and suggestions, but nothing ever seemed to come of them, and as time passed we realised that very little was being achieved. Michael was a lovely guy but he was just a bit lost as to what to do with us. But it wasn't all wasted time. During our time with him he did get us slots on *The Old Grey Whistle Test* and *Saturday Superstore*. This was around the time we were promoting our second single, 'Playground Of Privilege', which was released on Arista. We had parted company with Red Bus and been signed to BMG Records by a well-loved cigar-smoking character named Bryan Morrison.

'Playground Of Privilege' managed to get into the lower regions of the charts but it was very obvious to us now that guitar based bands were seriously on the wane. We rounded off 1985 by releasing our third single, 'You Won't Stop'. Both songs did get some airplay but back then if a song wasn't getting onto the Radio One playlist it was pretty much doomed for commercial failure. Radio One didn't put 'You Won't Stop' on their playlist.

It was all very frustrating because as soon as one record was released we had to start looking around for another record company to put out the next. Those one-record deals certainly had their problems. We carried on playing gigs regardless, selling out shows and getting a great response. This was always what I enjoyed most. It was very different to The Jam, not least because there were five members in Time UK. Unfortunately, like the record promotion, or lack of it, there was no proper coordination behind the gigs either. We never got around to sorting out a proper tour. It felt more like we stumbled from one show to another.

I found that I had more time on my hands which was something I certainly never had with The Jam. I spent it doing up my house and even got some of the members from Time UK down to help out with the decorating.

It was a struggle at times to keep Time UK afloat but it was still enjoyable and we got to work with some brilliant people, one of whom was the legendary producer Tony Visconti. Tony was a New Yorker, Brooklyn – his autobiography *Bowie, Bolan And The Brooklyn Boy* is a must read – but he moved to London in the late sixties after working with Georgie Fame.

It was whilst Visconti was making London his new home that he connected with Marc Bolan, producing Tyrannosaurus Rex, which became T. Rex with Mickey Finn. Tony then produced their next seven albums, which included the hugely successful *Electric Warrior*. He also worked on several David Bowie albums and most recently produced Bowie's *The Next Day* album. I don't recall how Time UK and Tony got together but we went to meet him and start some recordings at his Good Earth Studios in Dean Street in Soho. We did our second single, 'Playground Of Privilege'/'Puppets Don't Bleed', with Tony. I'm surprised that we even got through the recordings in the allocated time because we seemed to spend most of it asking him questions about working with Bolan and Bowie. He had a big glass-topped coffee table in his studio and underneath it he kept loads of photographs, Polaroids of people that he'd worked with in the studio. It was fascinating going through them.

I do remember that Tony was a bit miffed that he hadn't been offered the job on an album that Bowie was working on. It seemed like he felt he should have been given that album to do. Producers can be a bit like that. I had seen it before with Nigel Gray who had produced 'You Won't Stop' for us. He had worked on the first recordings by The Police but hadn't been offered the next album. Mind you, changing producers is not unusual. We changed producers with The Jam, first off with Chris Parry and Pete Wilson then Vic Coppersmith then back to Pete Wilson.

The mechanical process of recording is the same from one producer to the next but each brings their own unique approach and experience to the task in hand. And Tony did just that on 'Playground Of Privilege'. Looking back, I wish I had been able to spend more time working with Tony.

CHAPTER TWELVE

'You Won't Stop' backed with 'Further From Heaven' was Time UK's third and final single and although the gigs were still going well the interest from the record companies just wasn't there. It was frustrating that we couldn't release an album. The timing of this and my growing interest in the recording process side of things led me to start up my own studio and business, which I called Arkentide Ltd and established in premises in Liverpool Street in the Islington area of London.

It wasn't the last that anyone heard of Time UK though. In 2002 Dizzy at Detour Records released a compilation album called *One More Time*. I had collected together all the tapes that I could find of the Time UK masters, including different takes of the singles, both the A and B-sides, plus recordings that had never been released. Some of the material I had on Betamax in a digital format and some we had to rescue from cassette, many of which had never been mixed down properly, so we had to work through everything to find the best audio quality.

Me and Jimmy Edwards got in contact with a guy called Geoff who had worked with Genesis and Phil Collins and he had access to a studio called The Farm at Chiddingfold in Surrey where he had worked before. So we took up his offer and went down there to master all those Time UK songs. Then we had to set about getting the permissions from all the various record companies that Time UK had been involved with.

Then there was Mark Johnson from Unicorn Records. Mark was an American who had relocated to the UK and become involved in organising mod shows around London. He had recorded one of Time UK's live shows in Lewisham and released it on Unicorn. Additionally, there were some demo recordings where Bruce Foxton had played bass on the tracks, a project that went under the name of Sharp. Some of the Sharp stuff had been released on vinyl via Mark's Unicorn Records but was not of the same quality as the Time UK releases.

For the Sharp project we included another mate of ours, a guy called Keith West. He was the composer of the song 'My White Bicycle', which had been released by the sixties psychedelic band Tomorrow. Featuring future Yes guitarist Steve Howe, they were one of the more interesting bands from that era; part of the UFO Club scene, supported by DJ John Peel on his *Perfumed Garden* radio show and also producer Joe Boyd, who wrote a book about the era which he called *White Bicycles*.

We pulled in a collection of different musicians for the Sharp demos. We had no real direction at the time, it was just something to do and we had no expectations as to what might come from it. Bruce and Keith were involved and it was a bit of an afterthought to include those songs onto the *One More Time* album. Sadly, Time UK's guitarist, Ray Simone, died in 2012 following a lengthy illness.

Those Sharp demos were recorded at my Arkentide Studios and it was great to be working with Bruce again after a few years apart. There would be a much longer break before we played together again many years later.

The studio idea had been in the back of my mind for a few years. During my time with The Jam I had loved to play live but I had also really enjoyed being in the studio. Recording equipment fascinated me, and following studio sessions with The Jam I would take home quarter-inch tapes as reference, running order of albums, check mixes etc. I owned a quarter-inch tape machine, but Paul and Bruce used to take home cassettes.

I had befriended a guy called George Chambers who had worked as a tape operator at Townhouse Studios, and I approached him to help me source the premises and the equipment and soundproofing that would be needed.

We got the business up and running and work came in, mostly for record companies and independent bands. Some of the sound screens we had were supposedly used for the wedding of Princess Diana and Prince Charles in 1981, but whether this was true or not, I don't know. It did make a good conversation piece. The organisers had hung up loads of giant baffles around St Paul's Cathedral, and after the wedding they sold these baffles to a company called Larkings that specialised in professional sound recording equipment and fittings. Larkings put wheels on them and they were great big 6 ft padded blocks that absorbed sound and so great to use in a studio.

One of the bands that came through the studio was The Family Cat, based not far away in Stoke Newington although I think most of the members were from the West Country. They never really managed to break into the baggy scene, along with the likes of Inspiral Carpets and the Charlatans but did have a few successes in the indie charts. We even did some voiceovers for General Electric, and did a fair bit of bhangra music too. Many of the acts would come over to the UK to record their stuff with us and then send it back to India. Lots of it was used in Bollywood movies and shows. We had some Turkish acts too. The music had been recorded in Turkey on small 16-track machines and, because we had one, they could send it to us for mixing and recording the lead vocalist. The studio engineers certainly had some issues with the language barrier at times however.

We would do anything that the recording studio could be put to use for. But again, things seemed to be on the change. I had built the studio as a straightforward studio for live bands and the equipment in Arkentide catered for this, but computer technology had advanced and MIDI programs (musical instrument digital interface) were opening up new ways of recording.

I had to adapt the studio and this led to me going into partnership with Jim Hawkins, the drummer in a band called Strider. Jim was a bit of a wiz with keyboards, Fairlight machines and that sort of technology. Fairlight CMI (computer musical instrument) was designed in 1979 by Peter Vogel and Kim Ryrie; it was the earliest digital sampling synthesizer and became really popular in the mid-eighties. In the beginning this sort of equipment was really expensive, maybe £80,000, but then within a few years, with cheaper computers the same Fairlight dropped in value.

I had several studio engineers who were good with this sort of thing. Mike Spencer was exceptional with a real ear for the music and a grasp of the various programs, Cubase, Steinberg etc. He could find his way around all these MIDI technologies with ease. Since working at Arkentide Mike has worked with Kylie Minogue, Emeli Sandé and Jamiroquai. I learnt a great deal from people like Jim and Mike and for a while I had a guy called Jez Prior working at Arkentide too. Although I wasn't directly involved with any of the engineering work in Arkentide I was interested in everything that came through the studio and what was going on.

I was able to keep the studio up and running for a few years but the world was changing fast and it was hard to keep up. Plus I was having some difficulties with the landlord who owned the premises where Arkentide was located. The lease was up for review and the landlord wanted four times as much in rent. It just wasn't a viable option for me to keep the studio and the business running, so I made the decision to get out.

As a result I had to get rid of all this studio equipment. It was disappointing to have to wind down the studio, as it was something I thought had potential and that I was interested in doing. On a positive note though, I didn't miss the journey from Sunningdale to Islington that I did day in and day out, although for a time the studio manager Lee Ricard took me to and from the studio each day on the company car which was actually a Kawasaki 600 on which I rode pinion. Sadly, Arkentide was over by 1990.

Another band that recorded at Arkentide was The Highliners, formed in 1984 by Luke Morgan and Chris Finch. They emerged through the psychobilly scene and were regulars at John Curd's Klub Foot nights at the Clarendon Hotel, in Hammersmith, alongside The Meteors and The Guana Batz. The Highliners were introduced to me by a psychobilly fan who used to come into Arkentide to gain studio experience. He told me they had some half-finished recordings they couldn't get back from a recording studio because the bill had not been paid and the studio wouldn't release the tapes until the account was settled. The studio was in Wales, and what had happened was that their record company had run out of money and couldn't pay up. I offered to get involved by negotiating with the studio so I drove down to Wales to meet with the owners. Up until this point, all I knew about The Highliners was that they'd had a single out called 'Henry The Wasp', had a residency on the Channel 4 Show comedy *Wave Length* and had featured at the Klub Foot.

Phil Tennant and Neil O'Connor had been brought in to produce the Highliners album, and had done a really great job, most of the recording was complete but it hadn't been mixed. For obvious reasons the band wanted their album finished and released. The studio was still owed something in the region of seven grand, so I offered them £500 for the three two-inch tapes they had. The tapes alone had a shelf value of just over £300 back then. The studio rejected my offer, saying they could wipe the tapes clean and re-use them. Doing this, of course, meant that all the Highliners' work would be lost. I told the studio that I understood their position and regretted that they hadn't been paid, adding that I simply didn't have seven grand to give them either. We couldn't move forward and I drove back to Surrey frustrated and disappointed.

I slept on what had happened and decided to have another go at getting those tapes back. A solicitor friend drafted a letter warning the studio's owners that if they deleted what was on the tape they could be liable to be sued. The argument was that the tapes might contain a potential number one record. The solicitor explained that the studio could be held responsible for destroying someone's intellectual property, and the rub was that it didn't matter if the tapes had been paid for or not.

The studio responded by informing me that they still weren't prepared to release the tapes but would, instead, simply keep the tapes safe and sound on a shelf… forever or until I produced the seven grand. I replied, 'Well OK, but I'll drive down to you every month just to make sure those tapes are still safe.' They didn't believe me, but that's exactly what I did. I showed up on their doorstep a month later. At the time they had a heavy rock band recording who couldn't understand what was happening as I demanded that the tapes be taken off the shelf and run through the machine, just so I could check that they had not been wiped clean.

And then I did the same the next month and when I got there they told me that they were now prepared to take my initial offer of £500. So I handed over the money and took The Highliners' tapes back to my studio and Mike Spencer set about finishing the recording and mixing down the album. Once this was done I negotiated a deal with Razor Records and the album, *Bound For Glory*, was released.

The Highliners had their album and they were ready to promote it, but the band's drummer, Ginger (Steve Meadham), who had also been the drummer in The Meteors, left. The Highliners' drum stool was left vacant so they looked at me, 'You play drums! And you know the material!' they said. I had been listening to the songs for the past few weeks, so I knew the drum parts and songs pretty well; also I had organised two short tours with their agent to help promote the album, some university dates leading up to Christmas and straight after. So by default I ended up becoming the drummer in The Highliners and it was great fun to do. I have never played in such a fun band. The songs were good and the crowds were great; it was a really enjoyable time. And the band members were great people to work with, all of them were really good guys.

Unfortunately I never got around to doing any recordings with The Highliners, just the live stuff. They all had other commitments hanging around them as well, so it never felt like it was going to be a full time venture. Their guitarist Ben Blakeman would be off playing with The Cocteau Twins when they toured, but when this wasn't happening we would all get together and do some more shows. I worked this in with winding down Arkentide Studios and moving house, leaving my options open for whatever happened next. My relationship with The Highliners lasted for about three years until the shows thinned out. Chris, the sax player went into teaching and then I decided to walk away from music… for a while anyway.

But it wasn't the last that I would see of The Highliners. In 2010 Luke (Morgan) phoned me up to let me know that The Highliners were playing at the Goodwood Vintage Festival. It turned out that he had been given the job as curator of the fifties rock'n'roll stage and via this route had booked The Highliners as the headlining act. Luke invited me down, this time as a punter, so Lesley and I, along with our daughter and sister-in-law Sam, went down to watch another fun show.

It was good to see them and we got talking. I asked them if they had been receiving their royalties. They told me that they hadn't. I said I might be able to help them out (again). So I got involved with The Highliners once more.

...me UK at the Marquee. RICK BUCKLER ARCHIVES

...y Simone (RIP), Jimmy Edwards (RIP), Nick South, Fletcher Christian and Rick. RICK BUCKLER ARCHIVES

The Great White Kit. NEIL 'TWINK' TINNING

...ck, Alan Campbell, Tony Morrison, Ian Whitewood and Tim V.

...he Gift: Dave Moore, Russell Hastings and Rick Buckler.

The Gift at The Brook, Southampton. RICK BUCKLER ARCHIVES

he Gift, Newcastle. NEIL 'TWINK' TINNING

uce Foxton and Rick at The Junction, Cambridge, May 2007. GEOFF ROBINSON/REX FEATURES

Jason, Rick, Holly and Lesley, Jersey. RICK BUCKLER ARCHIVES

Bond Street Tube with Ian Snowball. TONY BRIGGS

...ick, Neil 'Twink' Tinning and Bruce Foxton at 'The Jam, Unseen' exhibition, photographs by 'Twink', October 3, 2007. STUART NICHOLLS/GETTY IMAGES

...ick with Ray Davies, London, February 2015. RICK BUCKLER ARCHIVES

Portrait of Rick by Danielle Tunstall. DANIELLE TUNSTALL

CHAPTER THIRTEEN

Once The Highliners came to a halt I found myself in another weird place. I also needed some money. A friend who owned a PA company – Merv The Swerve – asked me if I wanted to act as a drum roadie for a few of the acts whose tours he organised, including Lulu, The Three Degrees and Helen Reddy. I was offered the job because he presumed that I was sensible and reliable... I don't know about that but I certainly had the experience.

It was actually something that was nice to do and I got to see some 'behind the scenes' behaviour of the acts I was working for. For example I witnessed one act leave the venue, jump into a limousine clutching bunches of flowers, then drive around the corner, get out of the limo and dive into a Ford Escort in which to drive home while the limo went back to the yard. Doing the drum roadie work meant there was no pressure and I was getting a much needed income. Also the guys that I was on the road with were great fun.

Helen Reddy was great fun too, very down to earth and nice to be around. The Three Degrees (well two of the originals) were a laugh too. Everyone in the team seemed to enjoy playing practical jokes on one another. One tour manager who liked the sound of his own voice insisted on announcing the band, and the band egged us on to pull a stunt at his expense. So we stuck a condom over the end of the microphone. He went onto the stage, walked up to the mic and faced the audience (that was mostly made up of older women). He started to talk but his voice came out all muffled and quiet. Then he noticed the little teet hanging off the end of his mic and started to pull it off; only the condom kept stretching longer and longer until it eventually pinged off and went flying into the audience.

Another time we unwrapped all the bottles of champagne that were due to be brought out and presented to the band at the end of the encore, and replaced them with R. White's lemonade. Back in the dressing rooms the band was furious. We got told off for that. Then another night we decided to join in with their act. The Three Degrees used to do a dance routine on stage, similar to The Supremes, all lined up in a row, following each other's movements; only they had the stage back-lit rather than front which meant the lights would be shining up onto a large screen that served as their backdrop. So what we did was stand in between the lights and the large screen and attempt to mimic what the Three Degrees were doing. This meant our shadows would be projected but we'd be 12 feet high for all the audience to see. However, the Three Degrees couldn't see what we were doing and probably wondered what the startled, if not bemused, expressions were that the audience beamed back at them. We got told off for that too.

One of the bands that I worked with brought with them a musical director who acted as a conductor. A very talented American guy with an admirable reputation, he liked to make his presence felt and would often bark out orders to the band during soundcheck, always telling the drummer not to put a fill in at a certain point and so forth. One afternoon this guy went over to the sound engineer and started telling him that he had got the sound all wrong; the bass drum sounds rubbish and stuff like that. Of course, the sound engineer reacted and in moments both he and this MD were having a full-blown argument. Me and two other members of the road crew stood watching this from the wings, our arms folded and generally keeping out of the way. The argument then turned into pushing and shoving until it calmed a little and the sound engineer yelled, 'Look, how many number one records have you had?' The MD was a bit taken aback and huffed, 'Well, I haven't had any.' The sound engineer continued, 'So you're telling me that you've had no number ones in America, or the UK or Europe.' 'No,' replied the American, 'Anyway what's this got to do with anything?' 'Well, fuck you, there's more people on the road crew that have had more number ones than you,' and with that he glanced at me. The American stared hard at me but really couldn't make head or tail of what was going on. I guess he just wasn't a Jam fan.

During my time as a roadie I didn't especially miss playing the drums. One of my jobs was to set up the kits and when I did I used to have a little muck about. On one of these occasions one of the tour managers overheard me and came up to me and said, 'That's really good, any chance you can take over from the other drummer and do the show instead of him?' I declined.

I kept my hand in of course. During a break from being a drum roadie I did an album with a mate of mine called Brian Viner. We went back a long time and he was even one of the guys who auditioned for The Jam in the small room above the Red House pub in Woking when we were looking for a guitarist to replace Steve Brookes. Brian didn't get the job because he didn't really fit in with what The Jam wanted; he was a bit too much of a Ritchie Blackmore fan for us.

The album started out as bit of a home project for Brian. I said that I would help him out, and mentioned that I had recording equipment left over from Arkentide which he could use. I took the equipment around to his house and set it up, and I drummed on some songs for the album we produced that was called *The Fourth Wall*. It didn't only include me on drums; for convenience we also programmed drum machines. Backing vocals were provided by two women who sang in an Abba tribute act and they were fantastic. Another old friend of mine, Noel Jones, did the lead vocals and sounded like the lead singer of AC/DC. I helped out with the production and it was an enjoyable project to do.

Since I started to play the drums, whatever I have done has always involved music in the mix somewhere. I'm either directly involved playing drums, or I find myself around them? The nineties was all about Britpop and I watched that come and go. It was great to see the return of the guitar bands like Oasis, I could relate to this. Bands like Oasis moved the music industry away from the totally manufactured process and back to something more real again. I didn't really understand what the Blur/Oasis competition thing was all about though. I couldn't get that if you liked one of them you couldn't like the other.

But what bands like Oasis did was put the rock'n'roll industry back together. Guitar bands became popular again and a new generation of kids discovered the sort of bands that not only played their instruments but played them with attitude. In the mid-nineties that generation discovered The Jam for themselves, and this was almost 15 years after we had split up. As soon as Noel Gallagher was citing The Jam as one of his influences that was it, kids were off rummaging through their older brothers' and parents' record collections, just like we did in the sixties when we searched for rock'n'roll and discovered The Kinks and The Who.

It wasn't a bad thing when Paul Weller teamed up with Liam Gallagher, Steve Cradock, Damon Minchella and Steve White to record a version of 'Carnation'. This was the B-side to a version of 'Going Underground' that Buffalo Tom, a rock band from Boston, who had been going since the late eighties, recorded. That whole album, *Fire And Skill: Songs Of The Jam*, included different bands doing covers of Jam songs and was produced by Simon Halfon and released in 1999. It surprised me that acts like the Beastie Boys would do a version of 'Start' but I felt it was lifeless and didn't do the song any justice at all. Most of the other bands on the album were of the period: Reef did 'That's Entertainment', Gene did 'Town Called Malice' and Everything But The Girl did a good version of 'English Rose'.

Although I thought some of the album was absolute rubbish, it did serve to remind me that The Jam was still held in great respect among music lovers, and I think that respect still stands today. And this is something that leaves me feeling really proud. There was something about The Jam that distanced us from most other bands. We weren't stereotypical rock stars, like those bands that were massive in the seventies running around tearing up hotels with their outrageous haircuts. This was an important reason why fans, especially in Britain, related to us. We just didn't put on any airs or graces. We didn't need to.

By the time the Britpop thing had finished I was certainly aware that The Jam had a whole new breed of fanbase. A new Jam army had been turned on to the group through Oasis and a few others, and many of them were teenagers who hadn't even been born when The Jam was together; but they were discovering us now and liking what they heard.

Around the time I was working as a drum roadie I was also in the process of moving house. Back then the interest rates on mortgages were outrageous and Lesley and I needed to adjust and establish ourselves somewhere else. Also, Bruce and I were trying to sort out issues relating to unpaid royalties and rights going back to The Jam.

After a few months my finances settled down a bit and I decided to stop the drum roadie work and instead indulge myself in something from my past that I knew I would enjoy. I'd never forgotten making my first drum kit during the woodwork class at Sheerwater. I liked working with wood and I liked working with my hands and the timing to do something like this seemed perfect. I got in contact with a cabinet maker called John and tried to persuade him to take me on as a private student. It took some pestering on my part as he was working in Old Woking as an antique furniture restorer for a local dealer. But he did eventually give in and came round to my house twice a week to teach me the trade.

The more I saw of John's work the more I realised how little I knew and the more fascinated I became. I set up a workshop at home and set about acquiring the necessary tools. John would set me tasks to help me learn about the various techniques of furniture making and restoration. Before long we were restoring anything from chests of drawers to grandfather clocks. I was constantly expanding my own tool collection so I was always going to car boot fairs to hunt down a particular tool that was necessary for a specific task.

My workshop was soon bristling with a tool for every job and my skills were developing. I learnt about veneering, French polishing, turning, inlays and marquetry and cane seating and I loved doing it. I started to get some private commissions and I established a small network of others in the trade, traditional upholsterers, horological repairers and specialist suppliers for replacement escutcheons, ormolu and other brass work.

The work became more varied and knowledge of other fields such as gilding became essential. So I enrolled onto a short four-day gilding course in Hereford to familiarise with the techniques. The insight from this course was invaluable and opened up new areas to explore and work within. There's something so tangible about working with wood. You start off with something that looks a certain way but once you've finished with it, it can look so different. There's a real sense of satisfaction to be gained from it and I enjoy and respect the discipline of how wooden objects are crafted and made.

This country has a great legacy when it comes to working in the field of cabinet making. At certain times in history Great Britain has produced the best furniture in the world, and the process has evolved over the centuries through apprenticeships and different techniques. There was a time when an apprenticeship would take seven years, then you had to work on your own for seven years and then you could take on an apprentice for another seven years; so this process took 21 years to fulfil, a staggering achievement that reflects the quality and importance of this area of work. What it meant was that the methods involved in furniture making changed and evolved slowly. Antique dealers' familiarity with how a piece of furniture was manufactured enabled them to date and value an object.

The knowledge and interest in this area is all important. Take for example the great frost that spread across Europe at the beginning of the 18th century, which diminished the stock of walnut trees in Europe. In 1721 the British Parliament removed all import duties from timber brought into Britain from British possessions in the Americas, and as a result mahogany replaced walnut for the making of fine furniture. Tons and tons of Cuban and western dominion mahogany was imported into the country. Chippendale acquired some of this mahogany and it went on to be known as the king of mahogany.

When I attended a series of courses relating to furniture making and restoration it was a new experience for me. I heard that there was a college in Chichester in West Sussex called West Dean that took on a certain number of students. I applied because the college had a great reputation for teaching the top-end stuff and finer points of furniture restoration. Established in 1971 as a charitable foundation by a man called Edward James, the college focussed on keeping the old skills alive in areas such as book binding, silversmith skills and furniture making. I applied for full time entry into the college but sadly I was unable to afford the fees, so it never went any further.

I began to find that there was sometimes more work that I could handle. I often had several projects on the go at the same time, and I would go from making a set of chairs from scratch, or a bookcase, or anything that took my fancy really, to restoring a customer's furniture. I once made a walnut escritoire with quartered veneers and secret drawers. It took me far too long to complete, cost far too much in materials and it sold at a loss; but it was a true labour of love. Had I had the space to keep it I would have, but I didn't and it was a sad day for me when it went off to the auction rooms.

I listened to music as I worked on my furniture and was thankful that those nineties bands brought back something worth listening to. Up until that point, for a few years I couldn't even turn the radio on for the crap I was hearing. I also tuned into Classic FM and found myself discovering classical music, an appreciation for which I hadn't allowed myself previously. Classical records had never found their way into my personal record collection when I was growing up. It was hardly a case of Bowie, Bolan and Beethoven.

Working in my shed I needed some kind of background noise and I actually found a station that was playing nothing but birdsong. It was a test broadcast for what was to become Classic FM. I spent hours quite happily working in the shed listening to the noise of those birds tweeting. Then one day I tuned in and instead of hearing the sound of birdsong there was classical music... which at first I was gutted about. As the day went on some familiar pieces were played and I found myself liking what I heard. I wanted to hear more and learn more. I mean I had virtually no idea what a certain piece of music was called or who had composed it but Classic FM DJs would talk about who wrote the music and when and with whom, and they would give historical context to the music that I found really interesting. I also learnt that not all classical music was hundreds of years old, which to some extent was what I had assumed. Through Classic FM I learnt that such composers as Elgar and Ralph Vaughan Williams were not that old at all. Having once been at the forefront of the punk movement – although The Jam were never really punks – I found classical music quite a refreshing change.

During those cabinet making years I was filmed for a programme called *After They Were Famous*. Launched in 1999, it ran for five years and the episodes included people like Eddy 'The Eagle' Edwards, Steve Strange, MC Hammer and myself. The proposal was that I would do a 20-minute interview and the money they paid bought us a new boiler which we needed at the time.

Unfortunately, as so often happens with the media, a myth evolved that had little to do with reality. The TV people came round to my house to do the interview and see my workshop and at some point a cameraman walked off and stumbled across some old and discarded rota toms at the bottom of the garden that my kids had been playing with. This led to them making the assumption that I had turned my back on my career of drumming and The Jam and the music biz and left my drums to rot at the bottom of the garden. Which, of course, was ridiculous. The truth was that I had bought a set of rota toms towards the end of The Jam but had chosen to use only two of the eight in the set. The drums that I didn't use I gave to the kids and at some point they had made their way into the garden, and kids being kids they had probably just left or had hidden them somewhere and they hadn't been seen again until that nosey cameraman spotted them.

Another benefit of working at home was that I was able to spend a great deal of time with our two kids, Jason and Holly. From the workbench in my garden shed, I was able to watch them as they morphed from children to teenagers, something I certainly wouldn't have been able to do if I was still on the road with The Jam. I used to do the school runs because Lesley had her own job to do. Indeed, I did most of the ferrying around, just like any other dad, taking the kids to pageants and to play with friends. Looking back now I'm glad I had the time to do this. It wasn't something I fully appreciated at the time, but I do now and it's not something that all fathers can experience. My son is now in his late twenties and has his own life and my daughter is just finishing her last year at university, so we don't spend as much time together as we did when they were young. But this happens to all families as their children grow older.

It might seem odd to some but my kids grew up without entirely realising that their father had been in a band called The Jam. The first time my daughter realised it for real was when the 2006 Brits was televised. This was the year that Paul was given the Outstanding Contribution to Music award and while was on stage images from his career were displayed on the backdrop behind him. My daughter's mouth dropped when she saw one of The Jam. Funnily enough, up until that moment it simply hadn't really registered with her that I had been one of the members of a band that included Paul Weller.

Of course The Jam was over many years before my kids were born so they hadn't been around any of that stuff. For my son it didn't sink in until he was a teenager. He was with some friends that he had met at a Reading Festival and happened to mention that his dad had played drums in a band called The Jam. Apparently they all screamed, 'Fuck off, you're kidding' because they thought he must have been joking. They didn't believe him at first but he was able to produce some sort of proof for them and they were suitably impressed.

Before I knew it I had been working as a furniture restorer for almost 10 years. The time had flown by. Then one day someone asked me if there was a database for The Jam's career. It occurred to me that there wasn't and I started to think about all the information that I had in my attic, the tour programmes, itineraries, photos and so on. The more I thought about it the more I realised what I had. Along with my own collection I had a box packed full with things that my parents had collected and had given to me when they downsized.

My own interest in the internet had been growing, so I decided to build my own website to serve as a Jam archive. I liked the idea of having a site that could capture some of The Jam history. Enthused by the idea, I set about collating as much information, clippings and photographs as possible. I named the site thejamfan.net and it very quickly took off. It's now turned into a great reference point for the history of The Jam.

I started with a gig list, the official info about the albums and singles and just kept adding to it. I added the 'On This Day' section where you can click on a certain day from a certain year and it will say something like: '11th March 1982, The Jam take off on their European Transglobal Express Tour' or 'On 12th June 1977 The Jam headline a Queen's Silver Jubilee festival at Stamford Bridge, Chelsea'. There's another section called 'As I Recall' where Jam fans have sent me their personal memories about a gig or the time they met one of us. This section partly inspired the book *Thick As Thieves*. There's also a section I called 'Without Whom' that includes photographs of some of those that worked with the band across the years, people like Dave Liddle, Bob Jeffries or Chris Adoja. And there's an online shop where products such as books, T-shirts and music can be purchased from various retailers. It's a great site for Jam fans to browse around and it is official. I am still adding to the site on a daily basis, usually with contributions sent in by fans. There is always new stuff appearing.

Jam fans are always contacting me via the site to tell me about their Jam experiences, and though it's dropped off as a result of Facebook, when they contact thejamfan.net at least they know it's me, and this keeps the band/fan connection going, just as it did when the three of us were together. I like it that Jam fans share their memories with me and the site. It's interesting to look at the ticket stubs – especially the prices – and photos they have taken the trouble to scan and send me.

I sometimes get corrected too. Someone emailed me recently to tell me that I had left off a couple of gigs from the gig section. What's more, the anoraks are usually right in correcting me when I have made a mistake relating dates or events. It's not always clear-cut though: there are times when I'm told something about a gig or something that may have happened but I can't remember so I don't know if it did or didn't happen. There's been times when I have been sent a poster for a gig and had someone say, 'See this gig did happen', so I put it on the gig list, then someone else pipes up and says, 'Ah, but that gig got pulled', so I take it down again.

I don't mind being corrected; it's just part of what comes with having been in a band that split up over 30 years ago. Back then I just did the shows; it wasn't like I thought that I needed to remember this or that because 30 years down the line someone would ask me about it. It's probably the same for Paul and Bruce or anyone who has been in a band; I mean what sort of reply would someone get if they asked Keith Richards how a certain gig went in June 1967?

On the whole it's all good though, and I hear a lot of quirky things. I recently spent a weekend in Newcastle with my friend Paul, a photographer who lives there, and while we were out and about we passed Newcastle City Hall where The Jam had played years ago. The door was open so we decided to poke our heads inside to see what it was like now. All of a sudden some old boy appeared and asked what we were doing. I explained that I had played there many years back with The Jam. He listened, nodded, and then disappeared into an office, only to pop up again a few minutes later clutching an old book. We watched as he flicked through the pages until he found what he was searching for, the page where it showed the date when The Jam played. But what he was keen to point out was the level of ice cream sales. 'Ice cream sales?' I asked. I don't remember an army of Jam fans wandering around gigs licking ice creams. It turned out to be a code the venue used to monitor alcohol sales and nothing to do with ice cream at all. The old boy was kind to photocopy that page and that's on thejamfan.net somewhere. It all helps to trigger the memories of Jam fans.

The only thing that does annoy me is when I hear self-perpetuating myths such as why The Jam was called The Jam, as in it was because Paul noticed a pot of jam at the breakfast table one morning. Or there was something I read recently where Paul had supposedly played me some early Style Council tracks in 1983 to get my opinion; to which I allegedly replied, 'Are you taking the piss?' Well that certainly never happened. I mean I'm not keen on The Style Council and that's no secret, their sound just wasn't my cup of tea, but I never said that to Paul. Another rumour I heard recently was about From The Jam, the group I formed with Bruce in 2007. According to this, the reason I left From The Jam was because Paul Weller had finally met up with Bruce, after having nothing to do with him for many years. Both Bruce and I had tried hard to get Paul involved with From The Jam, even if it was only in a small way, but he rejected the idea, so some of the gossip that goes around doesn't even make sense. I do wonder why and where people get this stuff from sometimes. Then I see photos of Paul, Bruce and me, as we are today, photoshopped into one photograph together as if we are a band again. Apart from being funny, it's the falsehood of it all that annoys me, but it is easily ignored.

When I come across nonsense like that something in me reacts and I want to reply but thankfully Lesley steps in to remind me to let it go and forget about it. There are lots of stories about The Jam, about me and Paul, or me and Bruce or any combination of the band that are simply not true, never were and never will be, but some fans are convinced they are true, even though most are just the result of Chinese whispers. I do find this nonsense funny at times. It can be hilarious the way it goes around and around.

Once the Jam fan site was up and running it attracted some attention from all angles and I was soon asked to set up a website for some small businesses in my area. I agreed and this set me on another path that would last for about four years. I enjoyed it at first but the appeal soon wore off. It paid a wage and during the cold weather working indoors was much more preferable than being in my shed.

It was when I started to think about new kids discovering The Jam that I found myself remembering playing through the set list at The Jam's last gig in Brighton, each song that went by invoking the thought that this was possibly the last time I would play this song. Soon the idea formed in me that it would be great to revisit and play those songs again. After the furniture restoration and website building experiences I sort of realised that now would be a good time.

One afternoon I bumped into Russell Hastings. We had first met when I was hiring bands to play an annual event for thejamfan.net website. I organised a few of these events at places like the Guildford Civic. At the time he was playing in a band called Maximum High who played, amongst other songs, Who and Jam covers and I had hired them to play at one of my events. I had also seen Russell play support for an American Jam tribute act who called themselves All Mod Cons. I always thought it strange that the first big Jam tribute acts were Americans. I found out that they were doing a tour of the UK for the first time in ages. Newcastle was on their date sheet, so I decided to go and visit some mates in Newcastle and see All Mod Cons at the same time. This was the first time I had seen a band do Jam covers and I admit I did find it a bit weird.

I bumped into Russell and this was timely for me because at the time I was in need of getting some double-glazing installed and Russell did that as his day job. He offered to do it for me for mate's rates. One day when he was working in my home he asked me if I missed playing or ever thought about getting back into playing. He said, 'Well I know all The Jam songs cos I've been playing them for years in Maximum High. Why don't we do a bit of Jam?' I thought about it, agreed and The Gift evolved from there.

I also owe my returning to playing to Johnny Warman who would always badger me about playing more often. John had played with bands like Bearded Lady and The Mods and had also written songs over the years for Cheap Trick, Starship and Sabrina and even some for heavy rock acts House Of Lords and Asia. I had known John since The Jam days and have lost count of how many times he would remind us of the days when he was an original mod back in the sixties. Then Russell recruited Dave Moore on bass and we booked some rehearsal rooms and spent hours bashing out Jam songs. Dave's main instrument was guitar but he was a great all-rounder. At first I found it frustrating that my arms didn't respond as well as I knew they could; well, I hadn't played drums like this for years. But gradually it started to come back and slowly I got back up to speed.

We rehearsed up a set and booked some shows, starting with The Brook in Southampton. We had no real idea what we wanted to do or where we wanted to go but the shows went down really well, which surprised me. I just wasn't expecting the interest but at the time Paul Weller and Bruce Foxton weren't playing any Jam songs. I also investigated some of the Jam tribute acts, and there were a few now, getting a crowd.

I remember the build-up to the first gig we played as The Gift. We were all nervous. We had no idea if anybody would actually turn up. We had even chosen a venue that had regular live bands and we did this thinking a crowd would turn up just to see live music anyway, us or anyone else. As it turned out the place was full and it was a really good night. But yes, I personally found it to be very nerve racking but then I always found doing gigs to be nerve racking. Pressure before a gig is natural. Pressure can help to keep a focus and to get it right. And this has always been important to me.

I really enjoyed playing those Jam songs again and it wasn't that much different from playing them 20 something years earlier. The mechanics were just the same. The audience too, only they were much older, like me. There was something I really liked about re-connecting with those Jam fans.

What was nice was that people didn't turn up expecting to hear The Jam. We appreciated this because we weren't trying to be The Jam. We had no intentions of trying to emulate The Jam; we were simply just playing Jam songs because that's what we wanted to play. We had no sense whatsoever of copying anything or anyone. Besides how could I copy my own drum beat?

I remember when we were playing a show in Dublin, a little club below street level. It was the afternoon and we were soundchecking, only the doors upstairs had been left open and a passer-by had heard us, recognised the songs and decided to wander down to have a peek. He stood there watching us, grinning and tapping his foot along to the songs, thinking to himself that we were just another Jam tribute act. Then I saw his face change as he suddenly realised that it was me, an actual Jam member playing the drums. It turned out that his wife had let him out to go and watch some football game but he had been under strict instructions to be home for his tea. He immediately got on the phone to his wife and pleaded with her, asking that he be allowed to stay out for the night and watch the gig. He got permission and stayed for the show and he kept saying to us, 'This is my lucky day, this is definitely my lucky day.' The crowd at the show that night was great, full of energy and enthusiasm. And we had certainly made that man's day.

There were a few occasions, only a few, when someone would grab hold of me and ask why was I playing drums in a Jam tribute band. This used to make me a bit angry. It just wasn't the case, but they couldn't see it. The reason I chose The Gift as the band's name meant something to me personally. I considered it a gift to myself that I found myself being in a position where I was playing

Jam songs, songs that were very important to me and had been a big part of my life. I also thought it was a nice gift to the loyal Jam fans too. After all, those songs were important to them as well. There was also something poignant about the fact that The Gift was the last Jam album and sort of represented the end of the band. Using the name The Gift seemed to fit at that time.

As the months went by The Gift started to attract more and more interest and the venues got bigger and bigger and we started to travel further afield, including Europe. I loved it and found it to be great fun. I was enjoying playing Jam songs, playing to Jam fans, playing the venues, playing drums and playing with the other members in the band.

We had roped in the very competent Ed, the house sound engineer from the Brook, as our permanent front of house soundman, though the owners of the Brook weren't too happy that we had walked off with their top man. Russell drove the van and we all travelled together, staying at the cheapest hotels we could find unless we played near enough to home to drive back after the gigs. There was something about going back to basics like this that appealed to me. There has always been something about travelling overnight that I like too. Stopping at service stations for a drink and bite and seeing the night life and characters is like being part of a whole other world. There's something quite magical about this and, of course, it reminded me of travelling with The Jam. When you travel with a band there is a kind of bubble that's unique to the group you are in, and the rest of the world and what's going on doesn't matter at all. I don't think there are many situations in life that offer this opportunity but travelling and touring with a band is one of them.

What was also nice about that time with The Gift was that there were no pressures on us. It wasn't like we were getting demands and timescales from record companies. We were free to just have fun and enjoy what we were doing. We still had our own lives to lead and so we arranged most of our gigs just for the weekends anyway. This also meant that Russell and Dave could hold down their jobs to a certain extent, so they didn't have to put themselves under any unnecessary pressure. Plus we all got on really well which made being in The Gift easy and enjoyable.

Then Bruce Foxton appeared. Many of our shows were being booked by Mag who described himself as an 'Agent/Promoter'. One afternoon while we were hanging around after a soundcheck in Cardiff, I got a call from Mag. He suggested that as Bruce's band Casbah Club was the support act for the upcoming Guildford University show, I should ask him if he wanted to jump up during our set to do a couple of numbers. He had recently left Stiff Little Fingers and had started Casbah Club alongside Simon Townshend, Pete's younger brother, and Bruce Watson and Mark Brzezicki who had both been in Big Country.

I was still in touch in Bruce, so I called him and he agreed to get involved but would have to brush up a bit. On the night he joined us on stage for two numbers and the crowd loved seeing two members of The Jam playing together again. The Gift then had a few more gigs coming up and Bruce joined us again. This started to create a bit of a buzz and word started to get around. Over the next few months Bruce's joining us for two songs turned into three, then four, then five; Bruce playing bass and Dave Moore shifting onto guitar.

Casbah Club wasn't really happening. For whatever reason they weren't getting the interest or the shows and the group was grinding to a halt. It reminded me of those days back in the early seventies when Paul, Steve and myself wanted Bruce in The Jam but he didn't want to join because he was playing in his own band. But once Bruce realised that The Jam were getting regular gigs he wanted in and this became the same with The Gift. It was the same scenario, just in a different decade. But it was great for Bruce to get involved and become part of The Gift just as it had been when he became a member of The Jam. Then, as time went by and Bruce made a habit of playing a whole set with us, someone suggested we change our name, from The Gift to From The Jam.

CHAPTER FOURTEEN

From The Jam hit a period where we were finding it difficult to get shows. The initial transition going from The Gift to From The Jam went smoothly and we were all excited. We did tours of America and Australia and we were offered a second tour of the States but it didn't look like it was going to work out financially. As we looked at ways of trying to make it work and bring the costs down Dave Moore stepped up and suggested that if he didn't go From The Jam could work with just me, Bruce and Russell. As a three-piece it would certainly reduce the cost of flights and hotels and a local tour manager could be used instead of taking one with us. A second tour of the States was looking more viable but a mix-up by the tour manager over the profit and loss in dollars written as pounds occurred, a mistake that would have cost us dearly if we'd gone ahead with a second tour.

Another tour of Australia ran into similar issues. Touring in Australia requires flying to every town because of the distance involved, and off days between shows are a drain on a tour's income when you're staying in expensive hotels, although it's great to have the time to see the sights; not so good, though, if like Russell you need the money and not a holiday.

Up until this point things had been going well for the band in the UK and the tours in America and Australia were good to do but we didn't really make any money. Also, it was becoming clear that From The Jam could work without Dave in the band. I wasn't in favour of this. Although all the time The Jam were together, at least in their recording days, we never had a second guitar on the road with us, we had brass sections, keyboards and backing singers but never a second guitar. When we went into the studio Paul overdubbed guitar parts that, of course, couldn't be reproduced on stage but having Dave around meant that those extra guitar parts could be explored and incorporated into From The Jam's live performances. Also, Dave was a great guitarist and could pull off to a tee all of Paul's little guitar breaks. There was even a time when From The Jam brought in a keyboard player, which was essential for songs like 'Town Called Malice' and 'The Gift'.

So the second American and Australian tour didn't happen and we found ourselves cancelling more and more shows for a variety of reasons. This impacted on our relationship with some promoters and PR agents and in the end our own management. It was a very frustrating period. By September of 2009 I'd had enough and left. That was the end of From The Jam for me.

It was OK for a while but I found myself feeling like we were just treading water and going round and round. The bubble had burst. We had played the Hammersmith Odeon, done some great shows in the UK, toured in America and Australia and had created a bit of a buzz. We were offered another shorter UK tour the following year with a gig at the Shepherd's Bush Empire but the deal wasn't as great and things started to slip. Generally, it had become hard work, and what with the continuous cancellations and tantrums, I found myself reflecting on the situation and reviewing my position in it.

There was even a time when we made overtures to Paul Weller, inviting him to get involved in some way. We suggested that it may be good to just turn up to a gig one night, maybe play a couple of numbers with us. Paul wasn't interested and it wasn't going to happen. He said some things to the press about only wanting to look forward and not look back and that was fair enough. What I did think was a bit odd was that around that time he started to include more and more Jam songs in his own set. But I also thought it was great that he was starting to play more Jam songs again. After all, we had every entitlement to play those songs. People have such a hunger to hear them. They also want to hear either Paul, Bruce or me talking about The Jam. Yeah sure, sometimes we get a bit fed up talking about it but it's never going to go away and I, for one, have learnt to embrace it. So Paul didn't join us on stage. I know Bruce joined him on stage at one of Paul's gigs at the Royal Albert Hall. They performed 'The Eton Rifles' and 'The Butterfly Collector' together which I'm sure was a delight for the audience. And that's OK. Why not?

I think Paul also made some comment about From The Jam being or turning into a cabaret act and to be honest it did start to feel a bit like that to me too. It's not what I wanted and I even suggested doing some new material. Dave had some songs that we started with The Gift that we could have worked on. I would have loved to record some new songs but I think there was a lack of confidence within the band and the whole act was secure with a full Jam set. We were confident and settled with them. We knew exactly where we were but to go into uncharted territory with new stuff was a bit too much. We worried about what the audience would think too. We were concerned that the audience may think we were trying to be an extension of The Jam. It would have been great fun to be creative again but it didn't work out like that.

I think others in the industry connected to us also came to a realisation that we were just going round and round. They'd had their share and didn't see it going anywhere. Maybe it would have been different if we had recorded some new songs. Who knows?

The fans would love to see The Jam reform and there have been occasions over the years when approaches from promoters and agents have been made. I've heard all sorts of rumours about this person or that agency putting up vast amounts of money to see The Jam reform. But I think what generally happens is that the first person they approach is Paul and then Paul says 'No' and it doesn't go any further. As far as Bruce and I are concerned, there is no doubt that we would do it. The person they need to persuade is Paul and no one has been able to do that.

I can understand Paul's position. He has had and continues to have his own career and so why would he want or need to reform The Jam? Opinion amongst The Jam fans is divided. Some would love to see the three of us back together while others wouldn't, but if Paul had come and joined us on stage, even for just a couple of numbers, that would have been fantastic. At the end of the day I think it was a lost opportunity, but that was Paul's decision and that has to be respected, even if I don't necessarily agree with it. For me, resigning to the fact that Paul wasn't going to join Bruce and me on stage with us was just another reason to convince me that it was time for me to leave From The Jam.

I'm pleased we filmed two nights from a From The Jam gig at the London Forum in 2007 and released it on DVD the following year. There were some unnecessary issues with the sound and editing which sadly ate into any profits, but in the end we did get a DVD out of it.

However, there were many highlights while I was in the band. When we went to America my wife, Lesley, and Bruce's missus, Pat, travelled with us, and this actually meant we had some time to spend exploring New York together. Back in The Jam days, even though on many occasions Lesley and Pat travelled with us, we didn't have the luxury of sightseeing in the places we visited. Our wives came with us to America, Japan and even Jersey. We would organise the Jersey shows at the end of a tour so that we could then stay on for a few days afterwards and make a holiday of it in St. Helier.

Back in the Jam days Paul would take Gill with him everywhere, travelling with the band all over the world. I used to think back then that their relationship was at risk of burning out as having Gill with him all the time was effectively like Paul was taking his missus to work with him every day. And who does that? I'm sure at first, when it was young love, it was great for them, but as time went by

I could see things arising in their relationship. I remember hearing them have some really big arguments, and I was awakened in my hotel room several times by the sound of those two shouting at each other. There are a couple of great photographs from Twink's book where you can see that Paul and Gill are not speaking to each other in the morning because they'd had some bust-up the previous night. But that's what relationships are like. They are far from all smooth running. Taking your missus on the road can be tough. Being on the road for a hard working band can be difficult at the best of times.

Going to Australia with From The Jam was another highlight. As The Jam had never managed to tour Australia it was my first experience of visiting the country. The promoter's thinking behind this was that there was a fairly large community of ex-pats living in Australia that had arrived over the previous decades and they would remember and appreciate Jam songs. It was great to do but we found it very expensive. There were big gaps between shows that needed to be filled, and this often meant that a couple of days were spent hanging around the hotels, which was nice, like being on holiday, but we were spending money in the bars and so on. Our profits from the shows were used up having fun. When we returned to the UK and added it all up, we hadn't made that much money, and this was the principal reason why we didn't end up going back to Australia for a second tour.

We did some great venues though in the UK. One was headlining the Saturday night at one of the Camber Sands Scooter Rally weekenders, an event that has been going for years and takes over the Pontins holiday camp in Camber Sands. Organised by Robin Quatermain, the rally is attended by over 2,000 music fans who stay in chalets and park their scooters in any available space. The organisers put on bands and DJs across the weekend, including a dedicated northern soul room, a skinhead reggae room and one enormous room for the scooter sounds, so over the weekend there are bands covering all sorts of different genres from ska to mod to punk and DJs pretty much doing the same. There's a really wide stage and that's where we played on the Saturday night.

The room was packed full of fans aged mostly from 40 to 50 and beyond, all dressed in their best mod, rude boy, skinhead, scooterist regalia and they really got behind us. From The Jam was made for that type of audience and event. For some it would have been the closest thing they would experience to seeing The Jam. There were certainly plenty of people who would have been too young to have seen The Jam when we were an active band. Everyone seemed in good spirits, the energy was good.

After the gig we hung around and chatted to people before retreating to our chalet. Then in the morning we got up and spent some time looking around the record and clothing stalls. It's a really well organised event full of like-minded people. It was a good one to play at.

Once I had made the decision to leave From The Jam I found myself asking what was I meant to be doing now. After a short while the IF project kicked off. This came about because of my re-connection with The Highliners after the Goodwood Festival. I was still in contact with Dave Parsons, Sham 69 and Tim V, the new frontman who was also acting as their agent. Tim had experience in all aspects of managing bands, having once been the manager of The Tubes, an American band who had had a hit in the seventies with 'White Punks On Dope'. I spoke to Tim about helping get The Highliners some gigs, so over our cups of tea in the Millwall café just outside the football ground we discussed bands and gigs. The Highliners were still putting the line-up together and planning a new album to get the band back off the ground and Sham 69 were having their own problems too. As a result Tim mentioned an idea of his about putting together a band that had two drummers, and wanted to know if I would be interested in being one of them. I wasn't that excited by the idea at first but every time we would meet up he would run the idea by me again. Gradually the idea grew on me; after all it wasn't something that I had done before, playing in a band with another drummer.

The proposed line-up was Tim V on vocals along with Ian Whitewood as the other drummer and Tony Perfect. Tony had played with mod revival band Long Tall Shorty that Jimmy Pursey had discovered in the late seventies and introduced to Polydor Records. Al Campbell, who was also playing with Sham 69, was the bass player.

It was an interesting project and we had brand new material to work on, although we did throw in a couple of Jam numbers and 'David Watts' as well. We actually only ended up doing about 10 gigs but it was good fun, especially playing in an outfit with two drummers. It was a completely different experience to what I had been expecting. During rehearsals we would set up the drum kits so that we faced each other so we could see what the other was doing. Some things we did were intuitively right for a song and this was always good. Ian and I did discuss some sections of a song where we would agree that I would stop and he would carry on, on a fill or something, and vice versa. It wasn't actually that hard at all to work stuff out, and having eye contact on stage was of major importance. There are different disciplines required when there are two drummers in a band. When there's only one drummer that area is the drummer's domain and no one else can go near it, but when there are two they really have to lock in with each other. Ian is a really good drummer and between us we were able to produce something really effective.

Having two drummers does come with its problems though. For example, we could only play venues that had a stage wide enough to accommodate two drum kits, and we had to turn down some gigs because of this which was disappointing at times. When my kit is set up it stretches across an area of about eight feet and Ian's was the same. So already the stage had to be 16 feet wide before you start adding other band members with their instruments and amps. Ian and I worked well together and we could have made it more complicated, but we didn't want to go down the lines of turning it into something like Adam & the Ants or Genesis.

IF was put together quite quickly and we went on the road quickly too. In the meantime Sham were resolving their issues and in the end I turned to Tim and suggested it would be better if he,

Ian and Alan just concentrated on doing the Sham 69 thing rather than stretch themselves too thinly. The others kind of agreed and that was the end of IF.

Soon after IF finished I found myself helping out a talented young girl named Sarah Jayne who was brought to my attention by someone I met through clay pigeon shooting. I went to see her play at a small festival in Bisley and her singing impressed me. We got chatting and I offered her some advice on what she would need to get together to make any headway in the music industry. I told her to keep writing material and get herself down to as many open mic nights as she could because that was a good way to gain experience. There were some frustrating areas that we had to deal with, not least because she was too young for some venues.

Looking for places where Sarah could play I spoke with local promoter Vic Falsetta, and we put on a show in Guildford and invited another local band called The Brompton Mix to headline. I knew of the Bromptons and knew they would help to pull in a crowd. I put Sarah Jayne on in the middle of the billing and Root & Groove Element, a band from London, to kick the night off.

I liked the Bromptons and after that gig in Guildford I went to see them a couple more times. I discovered they had no one managing them so I ended up getting involved with them too. They were in that place that so many bands find themselves in; basically running around in all directions like headless chickens with no real direction to head in and no one to advise them. I thought I could help and throughout 2013 I tried to find them as many gigs as I possibly could. This included supporting Stiff Little Fingers, The Blockheads, The Members and the UK Subs.

I tried to get the Bromptons gigs outside of Woking, taking them to Southampton, Ipswich, Brighton, anywhere that provided the opportunity to play to a new crowd. They were great at getting gigs around Woking and they were building a following but they needed to widen their reach. This isn't easy to do for any band.

There are elements to managing a band that I like, but most of it is just aggro really. But it's aggro that I know. I had plenty of experience in this area. For example, when The Gift was happening, the three of us managed our own affairs. Organising rehearsals, transport, venues, ticketing and so forth takes a lot of thought and time. It's not rocket science but it's not easy either.

It's also quite challenging trying to get a band off the ground. In these days there is no scene as such, like the one when I was starting out. When The Jam were putting themselves about there was a whole culture that welcomed live music in pubs and clubs, especially around London but to a large extent this doesn't exist any more. It's as if there are two layers to what's available nowadays. There's the media layer that includes the internet and TV world and then there's the real world layer, the pubs and clubs where bands can cut their teeth. A band's job today is to try and find the ways to knit the two layers together.

It's very different to what it was like in 1977 at the time of punk. What bands and their fans did was brilliant, like creating our own fanzines and ways of attracting attention. We couldn't get into *Sounds* and *NME* at first, so DIY projects like *Sniffin' Glue* were created. Then the bands and the fans of those bands could write their own reviews. What bands do now is still a DIY thing but the difference is it has to be within an established set of boundaries, namely Facebook and Twitter.

I'm not saying that I think it's any harder for a band in today's landscape, but I do think the criteria are different. People's expectations are different, and in a lot of ways the attention span can be very short. The girls get criticised. I mean because of the fierce competition, they are wearing virtually no clothes in their videos. This gets them noticed and they can attract sales or hits to their web presence; and all through running around in some expensive, almost erotic, video and wearing a skimpy outfit. This is what sells their music. The formula can be glossy and polished. There appears to be little hunger for anything that is a bit gritty and not conforming to the industry. What doesn't fit in doesn't get a look in. Bands either have to play the game or they have no chance. I think for most bands, trying to make any money out of playing music is no different from when The Jam started out. We, after all, worked a lot because we were a covers band. When we were playing the pubs and clubs, week in week out, we weren't making enough money to live on that alone. I don't think anything has changed there. Most bands and musicians still struggle when it comes to money and making a living out of doing something that they love.

There's certainly very little money in the products that bands put out there. Sales of CDs have been down in recent years. What is new is that bands can access other outlets where they can sell their own products, downloads and merchandise, and they don't need to rely on any middlemen. But this often has its limitations, and can be frustrating for any artist. Any band can get a few T-shirts and CDs made up and flog them at their gigs or via their own websites, but it is hard work. There is room for everyone but it's worth keeping in mind that TV talent shows are, first and foremost, making a 'television programme' and although the acts are not all bad the transient nature does leave me feeling that it's not always best for everyone. The type of talent aired is often narrow.

Thankfully there is still a great deal of talent out there. They are still playing in the likes of the Dublin Castle or the Hope & Anchor but if they turned up at the door of those television shows they would get turned away. And they would probably be pleased about it too. At the end of the day live music will go on and survive.

OUTRO

From an early part of my life The Jam had a profound influence on all the different endeavours I became involved with and the group still touches many other lives today. Although I am quietly very proud of the longevity of what we achieved many years ago, there have also been many less public aspects before and since then and that means a great deal to me too. John Lennon said, 'Life is what happens while you are busy making other plans.' I am constantly reminded of the love people have for the band, whether they grew up with The Jam or have recently discovered the music. It certainly will remain a big part of my life.

The story of The Jam keeps on going on. There have been several deluxe versions of our albums released and from what I hear there are more in the pipeline. I know there is talk of a documentary being made about The Jam and even a film. There have been photo exhibitions and there's even talk of somebody considering setting up a Jam fan club again. I guess this is only possible because people have a deep love for what Paul, Bruce and me did. And that's great! That's entertainment!